CW00809956

Lord Chesterfield's Advice to His Son, On Men and Manners [Selections from the Letters].

Philip Dormer Stanhope

Nabu Public Domain Reprints:

You are holding a reproduction of an original work published before 1923 that is in the public domain in the United States of America, and possibly other countries. You may freely copy and distribute this work as no entity (individual or corporate) has a copyright on the body of the work. This book may contain prior copyright references, and library stamps (as most of these works were scanned from library copies). These have been scanned and retained as part of the historical artifact.

This book may have occasional imperfections such as missing or blurred pages, poor pictures, errant marks, etc. that were either part of the original artifact, or were introduced by the scanning process. We believe this work is culturally important, and despite the imperfections, have elected to bring it back into print as part of our continuing commitment to the preservation of printed works worldwide. We appreciate your understanding of the imperfections in the preservation process, and hope you enjoy this valuable book.

Corbould.   Heath.

Pity is a sense of our own misfortunes
in those of other people.

PITY.

CHESTERFIELD'S

(1694 – 1773)

ADVICE TO HIS SON,

ON

MEN AND MANNERS.

––––––––––

LONDON:

SCOTT, WEBSTER, AND GEARY,

36, CHARTERHOUSE SQUARE.

1836.

BODLEIAN
D
1 MAR 1954
LIBRARY

CONTENTS.

CONTENTS.

CONTENTS.

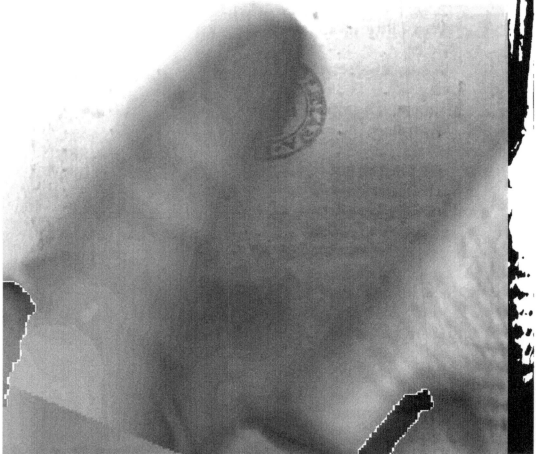

CHESTERFIELD'S

ADVICE TO HIS SON.

ABSENCE OF MIND.

An absent man is generally either a very weak or a very affected man; he is, however, a very disagreeable man in company. He is defective in all the common offices of civility; he does not enter into the general conversation, but breaks into it from time to time, with some start of his own, as if he waked from a dream. He seems wrapped up in thought, and possibly does not think at all; he does not know his most intimate acquaintance by sight, or answers them as if he were at cross purposes. He leaves his hat in one room, his cane in another, and would probably leave his shoes in a third, if his buckles, though awry, did not save them. This is a sure indication, either of a mind so weak that it cannot bear above one object at a time, or so affected that it would be supposed to be wholly engrossed by some very great and important object. Sir Isaac Newton, Mr. Locke, and, perhaps, five or six more since the creation, may have had a right to absence, from the intense thought their investigations required; but such liberties cannot be claimed by, nor will be tolerated in, any other persons.

No man is, in any degree, fit for either business or conversation, who does not command his attention to the present object, be it what it will. When I see a man absent in mind, I choose to be absent in body; for it is almost impossible for me to stay in the room, as I cannot stand inattention and awkwardness.

I would rather be in company with a dead man

than with an absent one; for, if the dead man affords me no pleasure, at least he shews me no contempt; whereas the absent man very plainly, though silently tells me, that he does not think me worth his attention. Besides, an absent man can never make any observations upon the characters, customs, and manners of the company. He may be in the best companies all his lifetime (if they will admit him), and never become the wiser: we may as well converse with a deaf man as an absent one. It is, indeed, a practical blunder to address ourselves to a man who, we plainly perceive, neither hears, minds, or understands us.

ATTENTION.

A MAN is fit for neither business nor pleasure, who either cannot or does not command and direct his attention to the present object, and, in some degree, banish, for that time, all other subjects from his thoughts. If, at a ball, a supper, or a party of pleasure, a man were to be solving, in his own mind, a problem in Euclid, he would be a very bad companion, and make a poor figure in that company; or if, in studying a problem in his closet, he were to think of a minuet, I am apt to believe that he would make a very poor mathematician.

There is time enough for every thing in the course of the day, if you do but one thing at once: but there is not time enough in the year, if you will do two things at a time.

It is a sure sign of a little mind, to be doing one thing and thinking of another, or not thinking at all. One should always think of what one is about; when one is learning, one should not think of play; and when one is at play, one should not think of one's learning.

This steady and undissipated attention to one object is a sure mark of a superior genius; as hurry, bustle, and agitation are the never-failing symptoms of a weak and frivolous mind.

Indeed, without attention, nothing is to be done : want of attention, which is really want of thought, is either folly or madness. You should not only have attention to every thing, but a quickness of attention, so as to observe, at once, all the people in the room, their motions, their looks, and their words ; and yet without staring at them, and seeming to be an observer. This quick and unobserved observation is of infinite advantage in life, and is to be acquired with care ; and, on the contrary, what is called absence, which is a thoughtlessness and want of attention about what is doing, makes a man so like either a fool or a madman that, for my part, I see no real difference. A fool never has thought ; a madman has lost it ; and an absent man is, for the time, without it.

In short, the most material knowledge of all, I mean the knowledge of the world, is never to be acquired without great attention ; and I know many old people, who, though they have lived long in the world, are but children still as to the knowledge of it, from their levity and inattention. Certain forms, which all people comply with, and certain arts, which all people aim at, hide, in some degree, the truth, and give a general exterior resemblance to almost every body. Attention and sagacity must see through that veil, and discover the natural character.

Add to this, there are little attentions which are infinitely engaging, and which sensibly affect that degree of pride and self-love which is inseparable from human nature, as they are unquestionable proofs of the regard and consideration which we have for the persons to whom we pay them. As, for example: suppose you invited any body to dine or sup with you, you ought to recollect if you had observed that they had any favourite dish, and take care to provide it for them ; and, when it came, you should say, ' You seemed to me, at such and such a place, to give this dish a preference, and therefore I ordered it. This is the wine that I observed you liked, and therefore I procured some.' Again : most people have their weaknesses: they have their aversions or their liking to such or such things. If we were to laugh at a man for his aversion to a cat or cheese (which are common antipathies), or, by inattention or negligence, to let them come in his way, where we could prevent it; he would, in the first case, think himself insulted, and, in the second, slighted; and would remember both. But, on the other hand, our care to procure for him what he likes, and to remove from him what he dislikes, shews him that he is at least an object of your attention, flatters his vanity, and perhaps makes him more your friend than a more important service would have done. The more trifling these things are, the more they prove your attention for the person, and are consequently the more engaging. Consult your own breast, and recollect how these little attentions, when shewn you by others, flatter that degree of self-love and vanity from which no man living is free. Reflect how they incline and attract you to that person, and how you are propitiated afterward to all which that person says or does. The same causes will have the same effects in your favour.

AWKWARDNESS

OF DIFFERENT KINDS.

MANY very worthy and sensible people have certain odd tricks, ill habits, and awkwardness in their behaviour, which excite a disgust to and dislike of their persons, that cannot be removed or overcome by any other valuable endowment or merit which they may possess.

Now, awkwardness can proceed but from two causes, either from not having kept good company, or from not having attended to it.

When an awkward fellow first comes into a room, it is highly probable that his sword gets between his legs and throws him down, or makes him stumble, at least; when he has recovered this accident, he goes and places himself in the very place of the whole room where he should not; there he soon lets his hat fall down, and, in taking it up again, throws down his cane; in recovering his cane, his hat falls the second time; so that he is a quarter of an hour before he is in order again. If he drinks tea or coffee, he certainly scalds his mouth, and lets either the cup or the saucer fall, and spills the tea or coffee in his breeches. At dinner his awkwardness distinguishes itself particularly, as he has more to do: there he holds his knife, fork, and spoon differently from other people; eats with his knife to the great danger of his mouth, picks his teeth with his fork, and puts his spoon, which has been in his throat twenty times, into the dishes again. If he is to carve, he can never hit the joint; but, in his vain efforts to cut through the bone, scatters the sauce in every body's face. He generally daubs himself with soup and grease, though his napkin is commonly stuck through a button hole, and tickles his chin. When he drinks, he infallibly coughs in his glass, and besprinkles the company. Besides all this, he has strange tricks and gestures; such as snuffing up his nose, making faces, putting his fingers in his nose, or blowing it and looking afterward in his handkerchief, so as to make the company sick. His hands are troublesome to him, when he has not something in them, and he does not know where to put them; but they are in perpetual motion between his bosom and his breeches: he does not wear his clothes, and, in short, does nothing like other people. All this, I own, is not in any degree criminal; but it is highly disagreeable and ridiculous in company, and ought most carefully to be avoided by whoever desires to please.

From this account of what you should not do, you may easily judge what you should do; and a due attention to the manners of people of fashion, and who have seen the world, will make it habitual and familiar to you.

There is, likewise, an awkwardness of expression and words, most carefully to be avoided; such as false English, bad pronunciation, old sayings, and common proverbs; which are so many proofs of having kept bad and low company. For example: if, instead of saying that 'tastes are different,' and that 'every man has his own peculiar one,' you should let off a proverb, and say that 'what is one man's meat is another man's poison;' or else, 'every one as they like, as the good man said when he kissed his cow;' every body would be persuaded that you had never kept company with any body above footmen and housemaids.

There is likewise an awkwardness of the mind, that ought to be, and, with care, may be avoided; as, for instance, to mistake or forget names. To speak of Mr. What-d'ye-call-him, or Mrs. Thingum, or How-d'ye-call-her, is excessively awkward and ordinary. To call people by improper titles and appellations is so too; as, my Lord, for Sir; and Sir, for my Lord. To begin a story or narration when you are not perfect in it, and cannot go through with it, but are forced, possibly, to say in the middle of it, 'I have forgot the rest,' is very unpleasant and bungling. One must be extremely exact, clear, and perspicuous in every thing one says; otherwise, instead of entertaining or inform-ing others, one only tires and puzzles them.

BASHFULNESS.

BASHFULNESS is the distinguishing character of an English booby, who appears frightened out of his wits if people of fashion speak to him, and blushes and stammers without being able to give a proper answer; by which means he becomes truly ridiculous, from the groundless fear of being laughed at.

There is a very material difference between modesty and an awkward bashfulness, which is as ridiculous as true modesty is commendable; it is as absurd to be a simpleton as to be an impudent fellow; and we make ourselves contemptible if we cannot come into a room and speak to people without being out of countenance, or without embarrassment. A man who is really diffident, timid, and bashful, be his merit what it will, never can push himself in the world; his despondency throws him into inaction, and the forward, the bustling, and the petulant will always precede him. The manner makes the whole difference. What would be impudence in one man is only a proper and decent assurance in another. A man of sense, and of knowledge of the world, will assert his own rights and pursue his own objects as steadily and intrepidly as the most impudent man living, and commonly more so; but then he has art enough to give an outward air of modesty to all he does. This engages and prevails, whilst the very same things shock and fail, from the overbearing or impudent manner only of doing them.

Englishmen, in general, are ashamed of going into company. When we avoid singularity, what should we be ashamed of? And why should we not go into a mixed company with as much ease and as little concern as we would go into our own room? Vice and ignorance are the only things we ought to be ashamed of; while we keep clear of them we may venture any where without fear or concern. Nothing sinks a young man into low company so surely as bashfulness. If he thinks that he shall not, he most assuredly will not, please.

Some, indeed, from feeling the pain and inconveniences of bashfulness, have rushed into the other extreme, and turned impudent; as cowards sometimes grow desperate from excess of danger: but this is equally to be avoided, there being nothing more generally shocking than impudence. The medium between those two extremes points out the well-bred man, who always feels himself firm and easy in all companies, who is modest without being bashful, and steady without being impudent.

A mean fellow is ashamed and embarrassed when he comes into company, is disconcerted when spoken to, answers with difficulty, and does not know how to dispose of his hands; but a gentleman, who is acquainted with the world, appears in company with a graceful and proper assurance, and is perfectly easy and unembarrassed. He is not dazzled by superior rank; he pays all the respect that is due to it, without being disconcerted; and can converse as easily with a king as with any one of his subjects. This is the great advantage of being introduced young into good company, and of conversing with our superiors. A well-bred man will converse with his inferiors without insolence, and with his superiors with respect and with ease. Add to this, that a man of a gentlemanlike behaviour, though of inferior parts, is better received than a man of superior abilities, who is unacquainted with the world. Modesty and a polite easy assurance should be united.

COMPANY.

To keep good company, especially at our first setting out, is the way to receive good impressions. Good company is not what respective sets of company are pleased either to call or think themselves. It consists chiefly (though not wholly) of people of considerable birth, rank, and character; for people of neither birth nor rank are frequently and very justly admitted into it, if distinguished by any peculiar merit or eminency in any liberal art or science. So motley a thing is good company that many people, without birth, rank, or merit, intrude into it by their own forwardness, and others get into it by the protection of some considerable person. In this fashionable good company, the best manners and the purest language are most unquestionably to be learned; for they establish and give the ton to both, which are called the language and manners of good company, neither of them being ascertained by any legal tribunal.

A company of people of the first quality cannot be called good company, in the common acceptation of the phrase, unless they are the fashionable and accredited company of the place; for people of the first quality can be as silly, as ill-bred, and as worthless, as people of the meanest degree: and a company consisting wholly of people of very low condition, whatever their merits or talents may be, can never be called good company; and, therefore, should not be much frequented, though by no means despised.

A company wholly composed of learned men, though greatly to be respected, is not meant by the words *good company*: they cannot have the easy and polished manners of the world, as they do not live in it. If we can bear our parts well in such a company, it will be proper to be in it sometimes, and we shall be more esteemed in other companies for having a place in that.

A company consisting wholly of professed wits and poets is very inviting to young men, who are pleased with it if they have wit themselves; and, if they have none, are foolishly proud of being one of it. But such companies should be frequented with moderation and judgment. A wit is a very unpopular denomination, as it carries terror along with it; and people are as much afraid of a wit in company as a woman is of a gun, which she supposes may go off of itself, and do her a mischief. Their acquaintance, however, is worth seeking, and their company worth frequenting; but not exclusively of others, nor to such a degree as to be considered only as one of that particular set.

Above all things, endeavour to keep company with people above you; for there you rise, as much as you sink with people below you. When I say company above you, I do not mean with regard to their birth, but with regard to their merit and the light in which the world considers them.

There are two sorts of good company: one which is called the beau monde, and consists of those people who have the lead in courts and in the gay part of life; the other consists of those who are distinguished by some peculiar merit, or who excel in some particular or valuable art or science.

Be equally careful to avoid that low company which, in every sense of the word, is low indeed; low in rank, low in parts, low in manners, and low in merit. Vanity, that source of many of our follies and of some of our crimes, has sunk many a man into company in every light infinitely below him, for the sake of being the first man in it. There he dictates, is applauded and admired ; but he soon disgraces himself, and disqualifies himself for any better company.

Having thus pointed out what company you should avoid, and what company you should associate with, I shall next lay down a few

CAUTIONS TO BE OBSERVED IN ADOPTING THE MANNERS OF A COMPANY.

WHEN a young man, new in the world, first gets into company, he determines to conform to and imitate it. But he too often mistakes the object of his imitation. He has frequently heard the absurd term of genteel and fashionable vices. He there observes some people who shine, and who in general are admired and esteemed, and perceives that these people are rakes, drunkards, or gamesters ; he therefore adopts their vices, mistaking their defects for their perfections, and imagining that they owe their fashion and their lustre to these genteel vices. But it is exactly the reverse ; for these people have acquired their reputation by their parts, their learning, their good breeding, and other real accomplishments ; and are only blemished and lowered in the opinions of all reasonable people by these general and fashionable vices. It is therefore plain that, in these mixed characters, the good part only makes people forgive, but not approve, the bad.

If a man should, unfortunately, have any vices, he ought, at least, to be content with his own, and not adopt other people's. The adoption of vice has ruined ten times more young men, than natural inclinations.

Let us imitate the real perfections of the good company into which we may get; copy their politeness, their carriage, their address, and the easy and wellbred turn of their conversation ; but we should remember that, let them shine ever so bright, their vices, if they have any, are so many blemishes, which we should no more endeavour to imitate than we would make artificial warts upon our faces, because some very handsome man had the misfortune to have a natural one upon his   We should, on the contrary, think how much handsomer he would have been without it.

Having thus given you instructions for making you well received in good company, I proceed next to lay before you, what you will find of equal use and importance in your commerce with the world, some directions, or

RULES FOR CONVERSATION.

TALKING.—When you are in company, talk often, but never long ; in that case, if you do not please, at least you are sure not to tire, your hearers. Take, rather than give, the tone of the company you are in. If you have parts you will shew them more or less upon every subject ; and if you have not, you had better talk sillily upon a subject of other people's than any of your own choosing.

LEARN THE CHARACTERS OF THE COMPANY BEFORE YOU TALK MUCH.—Inform yourself of the characters and situations of the company, before you give way to what your imagination may prompt you to say. There are, in all companies, more wrong heads than right ones, and many more who deserve than who like censure. Should you therefore expatiate in the praise of some virtue, which some in company notoriously want ; or declaim against any vice, which others are notoriously infected with ; your reflections, however general and unapplied, will, by being applicable, be thought personal, and levelled at those people. This consideration points out to you sufficiently, not to be suspicious and captious yourself, nor to suppose that things, because they may, are therefore meant at you. The manners of well-bred people secure one from those indirect and mean attacks ; but if by chance they are indulged in, it is much better not to seem to understand, than to reply to them.

TELLING STORIES, AND DIGRESSIONS.—Tell stories very seldom, and absolutely never but where they are very apt and very short. Omit every circumstance that is not material, and beware of digressions. To have frequent recourse to narrative betrays great want of imagination.

SEIZING PEOPLE BY THE BUTTON.—Never hold any body by the button, or the hand, in order to be heard out; for, if people are not willing to hear you, you had much better hold your tongue than them.

LONG TALKERS AND WHISPERERS.—Long talkers generally single out some unfortunate man in company to whisper, or at least in a half voice to convey a continuity of words to. This is excessively ill-bred, and, in some degree, a fraud; conversation stock being a joint and common property. But, if one of these unmerciful talkers lays hold of you, hear him with patience (and at least seeming attention), if he is worth obliging; for nothing will oblige him more than a patient hearing, as nothing would hurt him more than either to leave him in the midst of his discourse, or to discover your impatience under your affliction.

INATTENTION TO PERSONS SPEAKING.—There is nothing so shocking, nor so little forgiving, as a seeming inattention to the person who is speaking to you; and I have known many a man knocked down for a much slighter provocation than that inattention which I mean. I have seen many people who, while you are speaking to them, instead of looking at and attending to you, fix their eyes upon the ceiling or some other part of the room, look out of the window, play with a dog, twirl their snuff-box, or pick their nose. Nothing discovers a little, futile, frivolous mind more than this, and nothing is so offensively ill-bred; it is an explicit declaration on your part that every the most trifling object deserves your attention more than all that can be said by the person who is speaking to you. Judge of the sentiments of hatred and resentment, which such treatment must excite in every breast where any degree of self-love dwells. I repeat it again and again, that a sort of vanity and self-love is inseparable from human nature, whatever may be its rank or condition; even your footman will sooner forget and forgive a beating than any manifest mark of slight and contempt. Be, therefore, not only really, but seemingly and manifestly, attentive to whoever speaks to you.

NEVER INTERRUPT ANY SPEAKER.—It is considered as the height of ill manners to interrupt any person while speaking, by speaking yourself, or calling off the attention of the company to any new subject. This, however, every child knows.

ADOPT RATHER THAN GIVE THE SUBJECT.—Take rather than give the subject of the company you are in. If you have parts, you will shew them, more or less, upon every subject; and, if you have not, you had better talk sillily upon a subject of other people's than of your own choosing.

CONCEAL YOUR LEARNING FROM THE COMPANY.— Never display your learning, but on particular occasions. Reserve it for learned men, and let even these rather extort it from you than appear forward to display it. Hence you will be deemed modest, and reputed to possess more knowledge than you really have. Never seem wiser or more learned than your company. The man who affects to display his learning will be frequently questioned; and, if found superficial, will be ridiculed and despised; if otherwise, he will be deemed a pedant. Nothing can lessen real merit (which will always shew itself) in the opinion of the world but an ostentatious display of it by its possessor.

CONTRADICT WITH POLITENESS.—When you oppose or contradict any person's assertion or opinion, let your manner, your air, your terms, and your tone of voice, be soft and gentle; and that easy and naturally, not affectedly. Use palliatives when you contradict; such as, ' I may be deceived, I am not sure, but I believe, I should rather think,' &c. Finish any argument or dispute with some little good-humoured pleasantry, to shew that you are neither hurt yourself nor meant to hurt your antagonist; for an argument, kept up a good while, often occasions a temporary alienation on each side.

AVOID ARGUMENT IF POSSIBLE.—Avoid as much as

you can, in mixed companies, argumentative, polemical conversations ; which certainly indispose, for a time, the contending parties towards each other ; and, if the controversy grows warm and noisy, endeavour to put an end to it by some genteel levity or joke.

ALWAYS DEBATE WITH TEMPER.—Arguments should never be maintained with heat and clamour, though we believe or know ourselves to be in the right ; we should give our opinions modestly and coolly ; and, if that will not do, endeavour to change the conversation, by saying, ' We shall not be able to convince one another ; nor is it necessary that we should ; so let us talk of something else.'

LOCAL PROPRIETY TO BE OBSERVED.—Remember that there is a local propriety to be observed in all companies ; and that what is extremely proper in one company may be, and often is, highly improper in another.

JOKES, BON MOTS, &c.—The jokes, *bon mots*, the little adventures, which may do very well in one company, will seem flat and tedious when related in another. The particular characters, the habits, the cant, of one company may give merit to a word, or a gesture, which would have none at all if divested of those accidental circumstances. Here people very commonly err ; and, fond of something that has entertained them in one company, and in certain circumstances, repeat it with emphasis in another, where it is either insipid, or it may be offensive, by being ill-timed or misplaced. Nay, they often do it with this silly preamble : ' I will tell you an excellent thing ;' or, ' I will tell you the best thing in the world.' This raises expectations, which, when absolutely disappointed, makes the relator of this excellent thing look, very deservedly, like a fool.

EGOTISM.—Upon all occasions avoid speaking of yourself, if it be possible. Some abruptly speak advantageously of themselves, without either pretence or provocation. This is downright impudence. Others proceed more artfully, as they imagine ; forging accusations against themselves, and complaining of calumnies which they never heard, in order to justify themselves and exhibit a catalogue of their many virtues ;—'they acknowledge, indeed, it may appear odd that they should talk thus of themselves ; it is what they have a great aversion to, and what they could not have done, if they had not been thus unjustly and scandalously abused.' This thin veil of modesty, drawn before vanity, is much too transparent to conceal it, even from those who have but a moderate share of penetration.

Others go to work more modestly and more slily still ; they confess themselves guilty of all the cardinal virtues, by first degrading them into weaknesses, and then acknowledging their misfortune in being made up of those weaknesses. 'They cannot see people labouring under misfortunes, without sympathizing with and endeavouring to help them. They cannot see their fellow-creatures in distress without relieving them ; though, truly, their circumstances cannot very well afford it. They cannot avoid speaking the truth, though they acknowledge it to be sometimes imprudent. In short, they confess that, with all these weaknesses, they are not fit to live in the world, much less to prosper in it. But they are now too old to pursue a contrary conduct, and therefore they must rub on as well as they can.'

Though this may appear too ridiculous and *outre* even for the stage, yet it is frequently met with upon the common stage of the world. This principle of vanity and pride is so strong in human nature that it descends even to the lowest objects ; and we often see people fishing for praise where, admitting all they say to be true, no just praise is to be caught. One perhaps affirms that he has rode post a hundred miles in six hours: probably this is a falsehood : but, even supposing it to be true, what then ? Why it must be admitted that he is a very good post-boy ; that is all. Another asserts, perhaps not without a few oaths, that he has drunk six or eight bottles of wine at a sitting.

It would be charitable to believe such a man a liar; for, if we do not, we must certainly pronounce him a beast.

There are a thousand such follies and extravagances which vanity draws people into, and which always defeat their own purpose. The only method of avoiding these evils is never to speak of ourselves. But when, in a narrative, we are obliged to mention ourselves, we should take care not to drop a single word that can directly or indirectly be construed as fishing for applause. Be our characters what they will, they will be known; and nobody will take them upon our own words. Nothing that we can say ourselves will varnish our defects, or add lustre to our perfections; but, on the contrary, it will often make the former more glaring, and the latter obscure. If we are silent upon our own merits, neither envy, indignation, nor ridicule will obstruct or allay the applause which we may really deserve. But, if we are our own panegyrists upon any occasion, however artfully dressed or disguised, every one will conspire against us, and we shall be disappointed of the very end we aim at.

BE NOT DARK NOR MYSTERIOUS.—Take care never to seem dark and mysterious; which is not only a very unamiable character, but a very suspicious one too: if you seem mysterious with others, they will be really so with you, and you will know nothing. The height of abilities is to have a frank, open, and ingenuous exterior, with a prudent and reserved interior; to be upon your own guard, and yet, by a seeming natural openness, to put people off of theirs. The majority of every company will avail themselves of every indiscreet and unguarded expression of yours, if they can turn it to their own advantage.

LOOK PEOPLE IN THE FACE WHEN SPEAKING.—Always look people in the face when you speak to them; the not doing it is thought to imply conscious guilt: besides that, you lose the advantage of observing, by their countenances, what impression your discourse makes upon them. In order to know people's real sentiments, I trust much more to my eyes than to my ears; for they can say whatever they have a mind I should hear; but they can seldom help looking what they have no intention that I should know.

SCANDAL.—Private scandal should never be received nor retailed willingly; for, though the defamation of others may, for the present, gratify the malignity or the pride of our hearts, yet cool reflection will draw very disadvantageous conclusions from such a disposition. In scandal, as in robbery, the receiver is always thought as bad as the thief.

NEVER INDULGE GENERAL REFLECTIONS.—Never, in conversation, attack whole bodies of any kind; for you may thereby unnecessarily make yourself a great number of enemies. Among women, as among men, there are good as well as bad; and, it may be, full as many or more good than among men. This rule holds as to lawyers, soldiers, parsons, courtiers, citizens, &c. They are all men, subject to the same passions and sentiments, differing only in the manner, according to their several educations; and it would be as imprudent as unjust to attack any of them by the lump. Individuals forgive sometimes; but bodies and societies never do. Many young people think it very genteel and witty to abuse the clergy; in which they are extremely deceived; since, in my opinion, parsons are very like men, and neither the better nor the worse for wearing a black gown. All general reflections upon nations and societies are the trite, threadbare jokes of those who set up for wit without having any, and so have recourse to common-place. Judge of individuals from your own knowledge of them, and not from their sex, profession, or denomination.

MIMICRY.—Mimicry, which is the common and favourite amusement of little, low minds, is in the utmost contempt with great ones. It is the lowest and most illiberal of all buffoonery. We should neither practise it nor applaud it in others. Besides that, the person mimicked is insulted; and, as I have often observed to you before, an insult is never forgiven.

SWEARING.—We may frequently hear some people, in good company, interlard their conversation with oaths, by way of embellishment, as they suppose; but we must observe too, that those who do so are never those who contribute in any degree to give that company the denomination of good company. They are generally people of low education; for swearing, without having a single temptation to plead, is as silly and as illiberal as it is wicked.

SNEERING.—Whatever we say in company, if we say it with a supercilious, cynical face, or an embarrassed countenance, or a silly, disconcerted grin, it will be ill received. If we mutter it, or utter indistinctly and ungracefully, it will be still worse received.

TALK NOT OF YOUR OWN NOR OTHER PERSON'S PRIVATE AFFAIRS.—Never talk of your own or other people's domestic affairs: yours are nothing to them but tedious; theirs are nothing to you. It is a tender subject; and it is a chance if you do not touch somebody or other's sore place. In this case, there is no trusting to specious appearances, which are often so contrary to the real situation of things between men and their wives, parents and their children, seeming friends, &c. that, with the best intentions in the world, we very often make some very disagreeable blunders.

EXPLICITNESS.—Nothing makes a man look sillier, in company, than a joke or pleasantry not relished or not understood; and, if he meets with a profound silence, when he expected a general applause, or, what is still worse, if he is desired to explain the joke or *bon mot*, his awkward and embarrassed situation is easier imagined than described.

SECRECY.—Be careful how you repeat in one company what you hear in another. Things seemingly indifferent may, by circulation, have much graver consequences than may be imagined. There is a kind of general tacit trust in conversation, by which a man is engaged not to report any thing out of it though he is not immediately enjoined secrecy.

A retailer of this kind draws himself into a thousand scrapes and discussions, and is shily and indifferently received wherever he goes.

ADAPT YOUR CONVERSATION TO THE COMPANY.—Always adapt your conversation to the people you are conversing with; for I suppose you would not talk upon the same subject, and in the same manner, to a bishop, a philosopher, a captain, and a woman.

NEVER SUPPOSE YOURSELF THE SUBJECT OR LAUGH OF THE COMPANY.—People of an ordinary, low education, when they happen to fall into good company, imagine themselves the only object of its attention. If the company whispers, it is, to be sure, concerning of them; if they laugh, it is at them; and, if any thing ambiguous, that by the most forced interpretation can be applied to them, happens to be said, they are convinced that it was meant for them; upon which they grow out of countenance first, and then angry. This mistake is very well ridiculed in the Stratagem; where Scrub says, 'I am sure they talked of me, for they laughed consumedly.' A well-bred man seldom thinks, but never seems to think himself slighted, undervalued, or laughed at in company, unless where it is so plainly marked out that his honour obliges him to resent it in a proper manner. On the contrary, a vulgar man is captious and jealous; eager and impetuous about trifles. He suspects himself to be slighted; thinks every thing that is said is meant at him; if the company happen to laugh, he is persuaded they laugh at him, he grows angry and testy, says something very impertinent, and draws himself into a scrape, by shewing what he calls proper spirit, and asserting himself. The conversation of a vulgar man also savours strongly of the lowness of his education and company. It turns chiefly upon his domestic affairs, his servants, the excellent order he keeps in his own family, and the little anecdotes of the neighbourhood; all which he relates with emphasis, as interesting matters. He is a man gossip.

SERIOUSNESS.—A certain degree of exterior seriousness in looks and motions gives dignity, without excluding wit and decent cheerfulness. A constant smirk upon the face and a whiffling activity of the body are strong indications of futility.

ECONOMY.

A FOOL squanders away without credit or advantage to himself more than a man of sense spends with both. The latter employs his money as he does his time, and never spends a shilling of the one nor a minute of the other, but in something that is either useful or rationally pleasing to himself or others. The former buys whatever he does not want, and does not pay for what he does want. He cannot withstand the charms of a toy-shop : snuff-boxes, watches, heads of canes, &c. are his destruction. His servants and tradesmen conspire with his own indolence to cheat him ; and, in a very little time, he is astonished, in the midst of all these ridiculous superfluities, to find himself in want of all the real comforts and necessaries of life.

Without care and method, the largest fortune will not, and with them almost the smallest will, supply all necessary expenses. As far as you can possibly, pay ready money for every thing you buy, and avoid bills. Pay that money, too, yourself, and not through the hands of any servant ; who always either stipulates poundage, or requires a present for his good word, as they call it. Where you must have bills, (as for meat and drink, clothes, &c.) pay them regularly every month, and with your own hand. Never, from a mistaken economy, buy a thing you do not want, because it is cheap ; or, from a silly pride, because it is dear. Keep an account, in a book, of all that you receive, and of all that you pay ; for no man who knows what he receives and what he pays ever runs out. I do not mean that you should keep an account of the shillings and half-crowns that you may spend in chair hire, operas, &c. ; they are unworthy of the time and the ink that they would consume ; leave such *minutiæ* to dull penny-wise fellows; but remember, in economy, as in every other part of life, to have the proper attention to proper objects, and the proper contempt for little ones.

FRIENDSHIP.

YOUNG persons have commonly an unguarded frankness about them, which makes them the easy prey and bubbles of the artful and experienced; they look upon every knave or fool who tells them that he is their friend, to be really so; and pay that profession of simulated friendship with an indiscreet and unbounded confidence, always to their loss, often to their ruin. Beware of these proffered friendships. Receive them with great civility, but with great incredibility too; and pay them with compliments, but not with confidence. Do not suppose that people become friends at first sight. or even upon a short acquaintance. Real friendship is a slow grower, and never thrives unless engrafted upon a stock of known and reciprocal merit.

There is another kind of nominal friendship among young people, which is warm for the time, but luckily of short duration. This friendship is hastily produced, by their being accidentally thrown together, and pursuing the same course of riot and debauchery. A fine friendship, truly! and well cemented by drunkenness and lewdness. It should rather be called a conspiracy against morals and good manners, and be punished as such by the civil magistrate. However, they have the imprudence and the folly to call this confederacy a friendship. They lend one another money for bad purposes; they engage in quarrels, offensive and defensive, for their accomplices; they tell one another all they know, and often more too; when, on a sudden, some accident disperses them, and they think no more of each other, unless it be to betray and laugh at their imprudent confidence.

When a man uses strong protestations or oaths to

make you believe a thing, which is of itself so probable that the bare saying of it would be sufficient, depend upon it he deceives you, and is highly interested
in making you believe it, or else he would not take so
much pains.

Remember to make a great difference between com-
panions and friends; for a very complaisant and
agreeable companion may, and often does, prove a
very improper and a very dangerous friend. People
will, in a great degree, form their opinion of you upon
that which they have of your friends; and there is a
Spanish proverb which says, very justly, 'Tell me
whom you live with, and I will tell you who you
are.' One may fairly suppose, that a man who
makes a knave or a fool his friend has something
very bad to do or to conceal. But, at the same time
that you carefully decline the friendship of knaves
and fools, if it can be called friendship, there is no occasion to make either of them your enemies, wantonly
and unprovoked; for they are numerous bodies, and I
would rather choose a secure neutrality than alliance
or war with either of them. You may be a declared
enemy to their vices and follies, without being marked
out by them as a personal one. Their enmity is the
next dangerous thing to their friendship. Have a
real reserve with almost every body; and have a
seeming reserve with almost nobody; for it is very
disagreeable to seem reserved, and very dangerous
not to be so. Few people find the true medium;
many are ridiculously mysterious and reserved upon
trifles; and very imprudently communicative of all
they know.

GOOD BREEDING.

Good breeding has been very justly defined to be
' the result of much good sense, some good nature,
and a little self-denial for the sake of others, and with
a view to obtain the same indulgence from them.'

Good breeding cannot be attended to too soon or
too much; it must be acquired while young, or it is

never quite easy; and, if it is acquired young, will always last and be habitual. Horace says, *Quo semel est imbuta recens, servabit odorem testa diu* : to shew the advantage of giving young people good habits and impressions in their youth.

Good breeding alone can prepossess people in our favour at first sight; more time being necessary to discover greater talents. Good breeding, however, does not consist in low bows and formal ceremony; but in an easy, civil, and respectful behaviour.

Indeed, good sense in many cases must determine good breeding; for what will be civil at one time, and to one person, would be rude at another time, and to another person. There are, however, some general rules of good breeding; as, for example: to answer only, Yes, or No, to any person, without adding Sir, My Lord, or Madam (as it may happen), is always extremely rude; and it is equally so not to give proper attention and a civil answer when spoken to; such behaviour convinces the person who is speaking to us that we despise him, and do not think him worthy of our attention or an answer.

A well-bred person will take care to answer with complaisance when he is spoken to; will place himself at the lower end of the table, unless bid to go higher; will first drink to the lady of the house, and then to the master; he will not eat awkwardly or dirtily, nor sit when others stand; and he will do this with an air of complaisance, and not with a grave ill-natured look, as if he did it all unwillingly.

There is nothing more difficult to attain, or so necessary to possess, as perfect good breeding, which is equally inconsistent with a stiff formality, an impertinent forwardness, and an awkward bashfulness. A little ceremony is sometimes necessary; a certain degree of firmness is absolutely so; and an outward modesty is extremely becoming.

Virtue and learning, like gold, have their intrinsic value; but, if they are not polished, they certainly lose a great deal of their lustre: and even polished brass will pass upon more people than rough gold. What a number of sins does the cheerful, easy, good breeding of the French frequently cover!

My Lord Bacon says, ' That a pleasing figure is a perpetual letter of recommendation. It is certainly an agreeable forerunner of merit, and smooths the way for it.

A man of good breeding should be acquainted with the forms and particular customs of courts. At Vienna men always make courtesies instead of bows, to the emperor; in France, nobody bows to the king, or kisses his hand; but, in Spain and England, bows are made, and hands are kissed. Thus every court has some peculiarity, which those who visit them ought previously to inform themselves of, to avoid blunders and awkwardnesses.

Very few, scarcely any, are wanting in the respect which they should shew to those whom they acknowledge to be infinitely their superiors. The man of fashion and of the world expresses it in its full extent, but naturally, easily, and without concern : whereas· a man who is not used to keep good company expresses it awkwardly; one sees that he is not used to it, and that it costs him a great deal : but I never saw the worst bred man living guilty of lolling, whistling, scratching his head, and such like indecencies, in company that he respected. In such companies, therefore, the only point to be attended to is to shew that respect which every body means to shew, in an easy, unembarrassed, and graceful manner.

In mixed companies, whoever is admitted to make part of them is, for the time at least, supposed to be upon a footing of equality with the rest; and consequently every one claims, and very justly every mark of civility and good breeding. Ease is allowed, but carelessness and negligence are strictly forbidden. If a man accosts you, and talks to you ever so dully or frivolously, it is worse than rudeness, it is brutality, to shew him, by a manifest inattention to what he says that you think him a fool or a blockhead, and not worth hearing. It is much more so with regard to women; who, of whatever rank they are, are entitled, in consideration of their sex, not only to an attentive, but an officious good breeding from men. Their little wants, likings, dislikes, preferences, antipathies, fancies, whims, and even impertinencies, must be officiously attended to, flattered, and, if possible, guessed at and anticipated, by a well-bred man. You must never usurp to yourself those conveniences and *agremens* which are of common right; such as the best places, the best dishes, &c.; but, on the contrary, always decline them yourself, and offer them to others, who, in their turns, will offer them to you; so that, upon the whole, you will, in your turn, enjoy your share of common right.

The third sort of good breeding is local, and is variously modified in not only different countries, but in different towns of the same country. But it must be founded upon the two former sorts; they are the matter to which, in this case, fashion and custom only give the different shapes and impressions. Whoever has the first two sorts will easily acquire this third sort of good breeding, which depends singly upon attention and observation. It is properly the polish, the lustre, the last finishing strokes, of good breeding. A man of sense therefore carefully attends to the local manners of the respective places where he is, and takes for his models those persons whom he observes to be at the head of the fashion and good breeding. He watches how they address themselves to their superiors, how they accost their equals, and how they treat their inferiors; and lets none of those little niceties escape him, which are to good breeding what the last delicate and masterly touches are to a good picture, and which the vulgar have no notion of, but by which good judges distinguish the master. He attends even to their air, dress, and motions, and imitates them liberally and not servilely; he copies, out does not mimic. These personal graces are of very great consequence. They anticipate the sentiments, before merit can engage the understanding; they captivate the heart, and give rise, I believe, to the extravagant notions of charms and philtres. Their effects were so surprising that they were reckoned supernatural

In short, as it is necessary to possess learning, honour, and virtue, to gain the esteem and admiration of mankind, so politeness and good breeding are equally necessary to render us agreeable in conversation and common life. Great talents are above the generality of the world, who neither possess them themselves nor are competent judges of them in others; but all are judges of the lesser talents, such as civility, affability, and an agreeable address and manner; because they feel the good effects of them, as making society easy and agreeable.

To conclude. Be assured that the profoundest learning, without good breeding, is unwelcome and tiresome pedantry; and good breeding, without learning, is but frivolous; whereas learning adds solidity to good breeding, and goo. breeding gives charms and graces to learning; that a man, who is not perfectly well bred, is unfit for good company, and unwelcome in it; and that a man, who is not well bred, is full as unfit for business as for company.

Make, then, good breeding the great object of your thoughts and actions. Observe carefully the behaviour and manners of those who are distinguished by their good breeding; imitate, nay, endeavour to excel, that you may at least reach them; and be convinced that good breeding is, to all worldly qualifications, what charity is to all Christian virtues. Observe how it adorns merit, and how often it covers the want of it.

GRACES.

THE graces of the person, the countenance, and the way of speaking, are essential things; the very same thing, said by a genteel person in an engaging way, and gracefully and distinctly spoken, would please, which would shock, if muttered out by an awkward figure, with a sullen serious countenance. The poets represent Venus as attended by the three Graces, to intimate that even beauty will not do without. Minerva ought to have three also ; for, without them, learning has few attractions.

If we examine ourselves seriously why particular people please and engage us more than others of equal merit, we shall always find that it is because the former have the Graces, and the latter not. I have known many a woman, with an exact shape and a symmetrical assemblage of beautiful features, please nobody ; while others, with very moderate shape and features, have charmed every body. It is certain that Venus will not charm so much without her attendant Graces, as they will without her. Among men, how often has the most solid merit been neglected, unwelcome, or even rejected, for want of them ! while flimsy parts, little knowledge, and less merit, introduced by the Graces, have been received, cherished, and admired.

If you ask, how you shall acquire what neither you nor I can define or ascertain ; I can only answer, by observation. Form yourself, with regard to others, upon what you feel pleases you, in them. I can tell you the importance, the advantage, of having the Graces, but I cannot give them you.

We proceed now to investigate what these Graces are, and to give some instructions for acquiring them.

ADDRESS.—A man's fortune is frequently decided for ever by his first address. If it is pleasing, people are hurried involuntarily into a persuasion that he has a merit, which possibly he has not : as, on the other hand, if it is ungraceful, they are immediately prejudiced against him, and unwilling to allow him the merit which, it may be, he has. The worst bred man in Europe, should a lady drop her fan, would certainly take it up and give it to her ; the best bred man in Europe could do no more   The difference, however, would be considerable : the latter would please by his graceful address in presenting it; the former would be laughed at for doing it awkwardly. The carriage of a gentleman should be genteel, and his motions graceful. He should be particularly careful of his manner and address, when he presents himself in company. Let them be respectful without meanness, easy without too much familiarity, genteel without affectation, and insinuating without any seeming art or design. Men, as well as women, are much oftener led by their hearts than by their understandings. The way to the heart is through the senses; please their eyes and their ears, and the work is half done.

ART OF PLEASING.—It is a very old and a very true maxim, that those kings reign the most secure and the most absolute who reign in the hearts of their people. Their popularity is a better guard than their army; and the affections of their subjects a better pledge of their obedience than their fears. This rule is, in proportion, full as true, though upon a different scale, with regard to private people. A man who possesses that great art of pleasing universally, and of gaining the affections of those with whom he converses, possesses a strength which nothing else can give him; a strength which facilitates and helps his rise, and which, in case of accidents, breaks his fall. Few young people of your age sufficiently consider this great point of popularity; and, when they grow older and wiser, strive in vain to recover what they lost by their negligence. There are three principal causes that hinder them from acquiring this useful strength : pride, inattention, and *mauvaise honte*. The first I will not, I cannot, suspect you of; it is too much below your understanding. You cannot, and I am sure you do not, think yourself superior by nature to the Savoyard who cleans your room, or the footman who cleans your shoes; but you may rejoice, and with reason, at the difference which fortune has made in your favour. Enjoy all those advantages; but without insulting those who are unfortunate enough to want them, or even doing any thing unnecessarily that may remind them of that want. For my own part, I am more upon my guard as to my behaviour to my servants, and others who are called my inferiors, than I am towards my equals: for fear of being suspected of that mean and ungenerous sentiment, of desiring to make others feel that difference which fortune has, and perhaps, too, undeservedly, made between us. Young people do not enough attend to this; but falsely imagine that the imperative mood and a rough tone of authority and decision are indications of spirit and courage.

Inattention is always looked upon, though sometimes unjustly, as the effect of pride and contempt; and, where it is thought so, is never forgiven. In this article young people are generally exceedingly to blame, and offend extremely. Their whole attention is engrossed by their particular set of acquaintance, and by some few glaring and exalted objects of rank, beauty, or parts; all the rest they think so little worth their care that they neglect even common civility towards them. I will frankly confess to you that this was one of my great faults when I was of your age. Very attentive to please that narrow court circle in which I stood enchanted, I considered every thing else as *bourgeois*, and unworthy of common civility: I paid my court assiduously and skilfully enough to shining and distinguished figures, such as ministers, wits, and beauties; but then I most absurdly and imprudently neglected, and consequently offended, all others. By this folly I made myself a thousand enemies of both sexes, who, though I thought them very insignificant, found means to hurt me essentially where I wanted to recommend myself the most. I was thought proud, though I was only imprudent. A general easy civility and attention to the common run of ugly women and of middling men, both which I sillily thought, called, and treated as odd people, would have made me as many friends as by the contrary conduct I made myself enemies. All this, too, was a *pure partie*; for I might equally, and even more successfully, have made my court where I had particular views to gratify. I will allow that this task is often very unpleasant, and that one pays with some unwillingness that tribute of attention to dull and tedious men and to old and ugly women : but it is the lowest price of popularity and general applause, which are very well worth purchasing, were they much dearer. I conclude this head with this advice to you : Gain, by a particular assiduity and address, the men and women you want ; and, by a universal civility and attention, please every body so far as to have their good word, if not their good will ; or, at least, as to secure a partial neutrality.

Mauvaise honte not only hinders young people from making a great many friends, but makes them a great many enemies. They are ashamed of doing the thing that they know to be right and would otherwise do, for fear of the momentary laugh of some fine gentleman or lady, or of some *mauvais plaisant*. I have been in this case ; and have often wished an obscure acquaintance at the devil for meeting and taking notice of me, when I was in what I thought and called fine company. I have returned their notice shyly, awkwardly, and consequently offensively, for fear of a momentary joke ; not considering, as I ought to have done, that the very people who would have joked upon me at first would have esteemed me the more for it afterward.

Pursue steadily and without fear or shame whatever your reason tells you is right, and what you see is practised by people of more experience than yourself, and of established characters of good sense and good breeding.

After all this, perhaps you will say that it is impossible to please every body. I grant it ; but it does not follow that one should not therefore endeavour to please as many as one can. Nay, I will go farther, and admit that it is impossible for any man not to have some enemies. But this truth, from long experience, I assert, That he who has the most friends and the fewest enemies is the strongest; will rise the highest with the least envy; and fall, if he does fall, the gentlest and the most pitied. This is surely an object worth pursuing. Pursue it according to the rules I have here given you. I will add one observation more, and two examples to enforce it; and then, as the parsons say, conclude.

The late Duke of Ormond was almost the weakest, but, at the same time, the best bred and most popular man in this kingdom.—His education in courts and camps, joined to any easy, gentle nature, had given him that habitual affability, those engaging manners, and those mechanical attentions, that almost supplied the place of every talent he wanted; and he wanted almost every one. They procured him the love of all men, without the esteem of any. He was impeached after the death of Queen Anne, only because that, having been engaged in the same measures with those who were necessarily to be impeached, his impeachment for form's sake became necessary. But he was impeached without acrimony, and without the least intention that he should suffer, notwithstanding the party violence of those times. The question for his impeachment, in the House of Commons, was carried by many fewer votes than any other question of impeachment; and Earl Stanhope, then Mr. Stanhope and Secretary of State, who impeached him, very soon after negotiated and concluded his accommodation with the late king; to whom he was to have been presented the next day. But the late Bishop of Rochester, Atterbury, who thought that the Jacobite cause might suffer by losing the Duke of Ormond, went in all haste and prevailed with the poor weak man to run away; assuring him that he was only to be gulled into a disgraceful submission, and not to be pardoned in consequence of it. When his subsequent attainder passed, it excited mobs and disturbances in town. He had not a personal enemy in the world, and had a thousand friends. All this was singly owing to his natural desire of pleasing; and to the mechanical means that his education, not his parts, had given him of doing it. The other instance is the late Duke of Marlborough, who studied the art of pleasing, because he well knew the importance of it: he enjoyed and used it more than ever man did. He gained whoever he had a mind to gain, and he had a mind to gain every body, because he knew that every body was more or less worth gaining. Though his power, as minister and general, made him many political and party enemies, they did not make him one personal one; and the very people who would gladly have displaced, disgraced, and, perhaps, attainted the Duke of Marlborough, at the same time personally loved Mr. Churchill, even though his private character was blemished by sordid avarice, the most unamiable of all vices. He had wound up and turned his whole machine to please and engage. He had an inimitable sweetness and gentleness in his countenance, a tenderness in his manner of speaking, a graceful dignity in every motion, and a universal and minute attention to the least things that could possibly please the least person. This was all art in him—art of which he well knew and enjoyed the advantage; for no man ever had more interior ambition, pride, and avarice, than he had.

CHOICE OF AMUSEMENTS.—A gentleman always attends even to the *choice* of his amusements. If at cards, he will not play at cribbage, all-fours, or put; or, in sports of exercise, be seen at skittles, football, leapfrog, cricket, driving of coaches, &c.; for he knows that such an imitation of the manners of the mob will indelibly stamp him with vulgarity. I cannot, likewise, avoid calling playing upon any musical instrument illiberal in a gentleman. Music is usually reckoned one of the liberal arts, and not unjustly; but a man of fashion, who is seen piping or fiddling at a concert, degrades his own dignity. If you love music, hear it; pay fiddlers to play to you, but never fiddle yourself. It makes a gentleman appear frivolous and contemptible, leads him frequently into bad company, and wastes that time which might otherwise be well employed.

CARVING.—However trifling some things may seem, they are no longer so when about half the world thinks them otherwise. Carving, as it occurs at least once in every day, is not below our notice. We should use ourselves to carve adroitly and genteelly, without hacking half an hour across a bone, without bespattering the company with the sauce, and without overturning the glasses into your neighbour's pockets. To be awkward in this particular is extremely disagreeable and ridiculous. It is easily avoided by a little attention and use; and a man who tells you gravely that he cannot carve, may as well tell you that he cannot blow his nose; it is both as easy and as necessary.

CHITCHAT.—Study to acquire that fashionable kind of *small-talk* or *chitchat* which prevails in all polite assemblies, and which, trifling as it may appear, is of use in mixed companies and at table. It turns upon the public events of Europe, and then is at its best; very often upon the number, the goodness or badness, the discipline, or the clothing, of the troops of different princes; sometimes upon the families, the marriages, the relations of princes and considerable people; and sometimes the magnificence of public entertainments, balls, masquerades, &c. Upon such occasions, likewise, it is not amiss to know how to *parler cuisine*, and to be able to dissert upon the growth and flavour of wines. These, it is true, are very little things; but they are little things that occur very often, and therefore should be said *avec gentillesse et grace.*

CLEANLINESS.—The person should be accurately clean; the teeth, hands, and nails should be particularly so: a dirty mouth has real ill consequences to the owner; for it infallibly causes the decay, as well

as the intolerable pain, of the teeth ; and is very offensive, for it will most inevitably stink. Wash your teeth
the first thing you do every morning, with a soft sponge
and water, for four or five minutes, and then wash
your mouth several times.   Nothing looks more ordinary, vulgar, and illiberal than dirty hands, and ugly,
uneven, and ragged nails ; the ends of which should
be kept smooth and clean (not tipped with black),
and small segments of circles ; and, every time that
the hands are wiped, rub the skin round the nails
backwards, that it may not grow up and shorten them
too much.   Upon no account whatever put your
fingers in your nose or ears.   It is the most shocking,
nasty, vulgar rudeness that can be offered to a company.   The ears should be washed well every morning ; and in blowing your nose never look at it afterward.

These things may, perhaps, appear too insignificant
to be mentioned ; but, when it is remembered that a
thousand little nameless things, which every one feels
but no one can describe, conspire to form that *whole*
of pleasing, I think we ought not to call them trifling.
Besides, a clean shirt and a clean person are as
necessary to health as not to offend other people.   I
have ever held it as a maxim, and which I have lived
to see verified, that a man who is negligent at twenty
will be a sloven at forty, and intolerable at fifty years
of age.

COMPLIMENTS.—Attend to the compliments of con-
gratulation or condolence that you hear a well-bred
man make to his superiors, to his equals, and to his
inferiors ; watch even his countenance and his tone
of voice ; for they all conspire in the main point of
pleasing.   There is a certain distinguishing diction
of a man of fashion : he will not content himself with
saying, like John Trot, to a new married man, ' Sir,
I wish you much joy ;' or, to a man who has lost his
son, ' Sir, I am sorry for your loss ;' and both with
a countenance equally unmoved : but he will say in
effect the same thing, in a more elegant and less

trivial manner, and with a countenance adapted to the occasion. He will advance with warmth, vivacity, and a cheerful countenance to the new married man; and, embracing him, perhaps say to him, ' If you do justice to my attachment to you, you will judge of the joy that I feel upon this occasion better than I can express it,' &c. To the other, in affliction, he will advance slowly, with a grave composure of countenance, in a more deliberate manner, and, with a lower voice, perhaps, say, ' I hope you do me the justice to be convinced that I feel whatever you feel, and shall ever be affected where you are concerned.'

DICTION.—There is a certain language of conversation, a fashionable diction, of which every gentleman ought to be perfectly master, in whatever language he speaks. The French attend to it carefully, and with great reason; and their language, which is a language of phrases, helps them out exceedingly. That delicacy of diction is characteristical of a man of fashion and good company.

DRESS.—Dress is one of the various ingredients that contribute to the art of pleasing, and, therefore, an object of some attention; for we cannot help forming some opinion of a man's sense and character from his dress. All affectation in dress implies a flaw in the understanding. Men of sense carefully avoid any particular character in their dress; they are accurately clean for their own sake, but all the rest is for the sake of other people. A man should dress as well and in the same manner as the people of sense and fashion of the place where he is: if he dresses more than they, he is a fop; if he dresses less, he is unpardonably negligent: but, of the two, a young fellow should be rather too much than too little dressed; the excess of that side will wear off with a little age and reflection; but if he is negligent at twenty he will be a sloven at forty. It is of great importance that your clothes are well made and fit you, for otherwise they will give you a very awkward air.

The difference in dress between a man and a fop is, that the fop values himself upon his dress, and the man of sense laughs at it, at the same time that he knows he must not neglect it. There are a thousand foolish customs of this kind, which, as they are not criminal, must be complied with, and even cheerfully, by men of sense. Diogenes, the cynic, was a wise man for despising them, but a fool for shewing it.

One should not attempt to rival or to excel a fop in dress; but it is necessary to dress, to avoid singularity and ridicule. Great care should be taken to be always dressed like the reasonable people of our own age, in the place where we are, whose dress is never spoken of one way or the other, as neither too negligent, nor too much studied.

Awkwardness of carriage is very alienating, and a total negligence of dress and air an impertinent insult upon custom and fashion. Women have great influence as to a man's fashionable character; and an awkward man will never have their votes, which are very numerous, and oftener counted than weighed.

When you are once well dressed for the day, you should think no more of it afterward; and, without any stiffness for fear of discomposing that dress, you should be as easy and natural as if you had no clothes on at all.

DANCING.—Dancing, likewise, though a silly trifling thing, is one of those established follies which people of sense are sometimes obliged to conform to; and, if they do, they should be able to perform it well.

In dancing, the motion of the arms should be particularly attended to, as these decide a man's being genteel or otherwise more than any other part of the body. A twist or stiffness in the wrist will make any man look awkward. If a man dances well from the waist upwards, wears his hat well, and moves his head properly, he dances well. Coming into a room and presenting yourself to a company should be also attended to, as this always gives the first impression, which is often indelible. Those who present themselves well have a certain dignity in their air, which, without the least seeming mixture of pride, at once engages and is respected.

DRINKING OF HEALTHS.—Drinking of healths is now grown out of fashion, and is deemed unpolite in good company. Custom once had rendered it universal, but the improved manners of the age now consider it as absurd and vulgar. What can be more rude or ridiculous than to interrupt persons at their meals with an unnecessary compliment? Abstain, then, from this silly custom, where you find it disused; and use it only at those tables where it continues general.

ASSURANCE.—A steady assurance is too often improperly styled impudence. For my part, I see no impudence, but, on the contrary, infinite utility and advantage, in presenting one's self with the same coolness and unconcern in any and every company; till one can do that, I am very sure that one can never present one's self well. Whatever is done under concern and embarrassment must be ill done; and, till a man is absolutely easy and unconcerned in every company, he will never be thought to have kept good, nor be very welcome in it. Assurance and intrepidity, under the white banner of seeming modesty, clear the way to merit, that would otherwise be discouraged by difficulties in its journey; whereas barefaced impudence is the noisy and blustering harbinger of a worthless and senseless usurper.

HURRY.—A man of sense may be in haste, but can never be in a hurry, because he knows whatever he does in a hurry he must necessarily do very ill. He may be in haste to dispatch an affair, but he will take care not to let that haste hinder his doing it well. Little minds are in a hurry when the object proves (as it commonly does) too big for them; they run, they hare, they puzzle, confound, and perplex themselves; they want to do every thing at once, and never do it at all. But a man of sense takes the time necessary for doing the thing he is about well;

and his haste to dispatch a business only appears by the continuity of his application to it; he pursues it with a cool steadiness, and finishes it before he begins any other.

LAUGHTER.—Frequent and loud laughter is the characteristic of folly and ill manners: it is the manner in which the mob express their silly joy at silly things; and they call it being merry. In my mind, there is nothing so illiberal and so ill bred as audible laughter. True wit or sense never yet made any body laugh; they are above it; they please the mind and give a cheerfulness to the countenance. But it is low buffoonery or silly accidents that always excite laughter; and that is what people of sense and breeding should shew themselves above. A man's going to sit down, in the supposition that he has a chair behind him, and falling down upon his breech for want of one, sets a whole company laughing, when all the wit in the world would not do it; a plain proof, in my mind, how low and unbecoming a thing laughter is; not to mention the disagreeable noise that it makes, and the shocking distortion of the face that it occasions.

Many people, at first from awkwardness, have got a very disagreeable and silly trick of laughing whenever they speak; and I know men of very good parts who cannot say the commonest thing without laughing, which makes those who do not know them take them at first for natural fools.

LETTER WRITING.—It is of the utmost importance to write letters well; as this is a talent which daily occurs, as well in business as in pleasure; and inaccuracies in orthography or in style are never pardoned but in ladies; nor is it hardly pardonable in them. The Epistles of Cicero are the most perfect models of good writing.

Letters should be easy and natural; and convey to the person to whom we send them just what we would say to those persons if we were present with them.

The best models of letter writing are Cicero, Cardinal D'Ossat, Madame Sevigné, and Comte Bussy Rabutin. Cicero's Epistles to Atticus and to his familiar friends, are the best examples in the friendly and the familiar style. The simplicity and clearness of the letters of Cardinal D'Ossat shew how letters of business ought to be written. For gay and amusing letters there are none that equal Comte Bussy's and Madame Sevigné's. They are so natural, that they seem to be the extempore conversations of two people of wit, rather than letters.

Neatness in folding up, sealing, and directing letters is by no means to be neglected. There is something in the exterior, even of a letter, that may please or displease, and consequently deserves some attention.

NICKNAME.—There is nothing that a young man, at his first appearance in the world, has more reason to dread, and therefore should take more pains to avoid, than having any ridicule fixed on him. In the opinion even of the most rational men it will degrade him; but ruin him with the rest. Many a man has been undone by acquiring a ridiculous nickname. The causes of nicknames among well-bred men are generally the little defects in manner, elocution, air, or address. To have the appellation of muttering, awkward, ill-bred, absent, left-legged, annexed always to your name, would injure you more than you imagine; avoid, then, these little defects, and you may set ridicule at defiance.

PRONUNCIATION IN SPEECH.—To acquire a graceful utterance, read aloud to some friend every day, and beg of him to interrupt and correct you whenever you read too fast, do not observe the proper stops, lay a wrong emphasis, or utter your words unintelligibly. You may even read aloud to yourself, and tune your utterance to your own ear. Take care to open your teeth when you read or speak, and articulate every word distinctly; which last cannot be done but by sounding the final letter. But, above all, study to vary your voice according to the subject, and avoid monotony. Daily attention to these articles will, in a little time, render them easy and habitual to you.

The voice and manner of speaking, too, are not to be neglected: some people almost shut their mouth when they speak, and mutter so that they are not to be understood; others speak so fast, and sputter, that they are not to be understood neither: some always speak as loud as if they were talking to deaf people; and others so low that one cannot hear them. All these habits are awkward and disagreeable, and are to be avoided by attention; they are the distinguishing marks of the ordinary people, who have had no care taken of their education. You cannot imagine how necessary it is to mind all these little things; for I have seen many people, with great talents, ill received for want of having these talents; and others well received, only from their little talents, and who had no great ones.

SPELLING.—Orthography, or spelling well, is so absolutely necessary for a man of letters, or a gentleman, that one false spelling may fix a ridicule on him for the remainder of his life. Reading carefully will contribute, in a great measure, to preserve you from exposing yourself by false spelling; for books are generally well spelled, according to the orthography of the times. Sometimes words, indeed, are spelled differently by different authors, but those instances are rare; and where there is only one way of spelling a word, should you spell it wrong, you will be sure to be ridiculed. Nay, a *woman* of a tolerable education would despise and laugh at her lover, if he should send her an ill-spelled *billet-doux*.

STYLE.—Style is the dress of thoughts; and, let them be ever so just, if your style is homely, coarse, and vulgar, they will appear to as much disadvantage, and be as ill received, as your person, though ever so well proportioned, would, if dressed in rags, dirt, and tatters. It is not every understanding that can judge of matter; but every ear can and does judge, more or less, of style.

Mind your diction, in whatever language you either write or speak: contract a habit of correctness and elegance. Consider your style, even in the freest conversation and most familiar letters. After, at least, if not before you have said a thing, reflect if you could not have said it better.

WRITING.—Every man who has the use of his eyes and his right hand can write whatever hand he pleases. Nothing is so ungentlemanlike as a schoolboy's scrawl. I do not desire you to write a stiff, formal hand, like that of a schoolmaster, but a genteel, legible, and liberal character, and to be able to write quick. As to the correctness and elegancy of your writing, attention to grammar does the one, and to the best authors the other. Epistolary correspondence should be easy and natural, and convey to the persons just what we would say if we were with them.

VULGAR EXPRESSIONS.—Vulgarism in language is a certain characteristic of bad company and a bad education. Proverbial expressions and trite sayings are the flowers of the rhetoric of a vulgar man. Would he say that men differ in their taste, he both supports and adorns that opinion by the good old saying, as he respectfully calls it, that ' What is one man's meat, is another man's poison.' If any body attempts being *smart*, as he calls it, upon him, he gives them *tit for tat*, ay, that he does. He has always some favourite word for the time being, which, for the sake of using often, he commonly uses ; such as *vastly* angry, *vastly* kind, *vastly* handsome, and *vastly* ugly. Even his pronunciation of proper words carries the mark of the beast along with it. He calls the earth *yearth ;* he is *obleeged*, not *obliged* to you. He goes *to wards*, and not *towards* such a place. He sometimes affects hard words, by way of ornament, which he always mangles like a learned woman. A man of fashion never has recourse to proverbs and vulgar aphorisms ; uses neither favourite words nor hard words ; but takes great care to speak very correctly and grammatically, and to pronounce properly ; that is, according to the usage of the best companies.

CAUTIONS AGAINST SUNDRY ODD HABITS.—Humming a tune within ourselves, drumming with our

D

fingers, making a noise with our feet, and such awkward habits, being all breaches of good manners, are therefore indications of our contempt for the persons present, and consequently should not be practised.

Eating very quick or very slow is characteristic of vulgarity: the former infers poverty; the latter, if abroad, that you are disgusted with your entertainment; and, if at home, that you are rude enough to give your friends what you cannot eat yourself. Eating soup with your nose in the plate is also vulgar. So likewise is smelling at the meat while on the fork, before you put it in your mouth. If you dislike what is sent upon your plate, leave it; but never, by smelling to or examining it, appear to tax your friend with placing unwholesome provisions before you.

Spitting on the floor or carpet is a filthy practice, and which, were it to become general, would render it as necessary to change the carpets as the tablecloths. Not to add, it will induce our acquaintance to suppose that we have not been used to genteel furniture; for which reason alone, if for no other, a man of liberal education should avoid it.

To conclude this article: never walk fast in the streets, which is a mark of vulgarity, ill befitting the character of a gentleman or a man of fashion, though it may be tolerable in a tradesman.

To stare any person full in the face, whom you may chance to meet, is an act also of ill breeding; it would seem to bespeak as if you saw something wonderful in his appearance, and is, therefore, a tacit reprehension.

Keep yourself free, likewise, from all odd tricks or habits; such as scratching yourself, putting your fingers to your mouth, nose, and ears, thrusting out your tongue, snapping your fingers, biting your nails, rubbing your hands, sighing aloud, and affected shivering of your body, gaping, and many others which I have noticed before; all which are imitations of the manners of the mob, and degrading to a gentleman.

KNOWLEDGE OF THE WORLD.

WE should endeavour to hoard up, while we are young, a great stock of knowledge; for, though during that time of dissipation we may not have occasion to spend much of it, yet a time will come when we shall want it to maintain us.

HOW TO ACQUIRE A KNOWLEDGE OF THE WORLD.—— The knowledge of the world is only to be acquired in the world, and not in a closet. Books alone will never teach it you; but they will suggest many things to your observation which might otherwise escape you; and your own observations upon mankind, when compared with those which you will find in books, will help you to fix the true point.

To know mankind well requires full as much attention and application as to know books, and, it may be, more sagacity and discernment. I am, at this time, acquainted with many elderly people, who have all passed their whole lives in the great world, but with such levity and inattention that they know no more of it, now, than they did at fifteen. Do not flatter yourself, therefore, with the thought that you can acquire this knowledge in the frivolous chitchat of idle companies; no, you must go much deeper than that. You must look into people, as well as at them. Search, therefore, with the greatest care, into the characters of all those whom you converse with; endeavour to discover their predominant passions, their prevailing weaknesses, their vanities, their follies, and their humours; with all the right and wrong, wise and silly springs of human action, which makes such inconsistent and whimsical beings of us rational creatures.

NEVER SHEW A CONTEMPT FOR ANY ONE.——There are no persons so insignificant and inconsiderable but may, some time or other, or in something or other, have it in their power to be of use to you; which they certainly will not, if you have once shewn them contempt. Wrongs are often forgiven, but contempt never is. Our pride remembers it for ever. Remember, therefore, most carefully to conceal your contempt, however just, wherever you would not make an implacable enemy. Men are much more unwilling to have their weakness and their imperfections known than their crimes ; and, if you hint to a man that you think him silly, ignorant, or even illbred or awkward, he will hate you more and longer than if you tell him plainly that you think him a rogue.

MAKE NO MAN FEEL HIS INFERIORITY.—Nothing is more insulting than to take pains to make a man feel a mortifying inferiority in knowledge, rank, fortune, &c. In the first it is both ill-bred and ill-natured ; and in the two latter articles it is unjust, they not being in his power. Good breeding and good nature incline us rather to raise people up to ourselves than to mortify and depress them. Besides, it is making ourselves so many friends, instead of so many enemies. A constant attention to please is a most necessary ingredient in the art of pleasing ; it flatters the self-love of those to whom it is shewn ; it engages and captivates more than things of much greater importance. Every man is, in some measure, obliged to discharge the social duties of life ; but these attentions are voluntary acts, the free-will offerings of good breeding and good nature ; they are received, remembered, and returned as such. Women, in particular, have a right to them ; and any omission in that respect is downright ill breeding.

NEVER EXPOSE PEOPLE'S WEAKNESSES AND INFIRMITIES.—We should never yield to that temptation, which to most young men is very strong, of exposing other people's weaknesses and infirmities, for the sake either of diverting the company or of shewing our own superiority. We may, by that means, get the laugh on our side for the present ; but we shall make enemies by it for ever ; and even those who laugh at us will, upon reflection, fear and despise us ; it is ill-natured, and a good heart desires rather to conceal than expose other people's weaknesses or misfortunes. If we have wit, we should use it to please, and not to hurt: we may shine, like the sun in the temperate zone, without scorching.

STEADY COMMAND OF TEMPER AND COUNTENANCE.—There are many inoffensive arts which are necessary in the course of the world, and that which he who practises the earliest will please the most and rise the soonest. The spirits and vivacity of youth are apt to neglect them as useless, or reject them as troublesome; but subsequent knowledge and experience of the world remind us of their importance, commonly, when it is too late. The principle of these things is the mastery of one's temper, and that coolness of mind and serenity of countenance which hinder us from discovering, by words, actions, or even looks, those passions or sentiments by which we are inwardly moved or agitated; and the discovery of which gives cooler and abler people such infinite advantages over us, not only in great business, but in all the most common occurrences of life. A man who does not possess himself enough to hear disagreeable things, without visible marks of anger and change of countenance, or agreeable ones without sudden bursts of joy and expansion of countenance, is at the mercy of every artful knave or pert coxcomb; the former will provoke or please you by design, to catch unguarded words or looks; by which he will easily decipher the secrets of your heart, of which you should keep the key yourself, and trust it with no man living. The latter will, by his absurdity, and without intending it, produce the same discoveries, of which other people will avail themselves.

If you find yourself subject to sudden starts of passion, or madness (for I see no difference between them but in their duration), resolve within yourself, at least, never to speak one word while you feel that emotion within you.

In short, make yourself absolute master of your temper and your countenance, so far, at least, as that no visible change do appear in either, whatever you may feel inwardly. This may be difficult, but it is by no means impossible; and, as a man of sense never attempts impossibilities on the one hand, on the other he is never discouraged by difficulties: on the contrary, he redoubles his industry and his diligence; he perseveres, and infallibly prevails at last. In any point which prudence bids you pursue, and which a manifest utility attends, let difficulties only animate your industry, not deter you from the pursuit. If one way has failed, try another; be active, persevere, and you will conquer. Some people are to be reasoned, some flattered, some intimidated, and some teased, into a thing; but, in general, all are to be brought into it at last, if skilfully applied to, properly managed, and indefatigably attacked in their several weak places. The time should likewise be judiciously chosen: every man has his *mollia tempora*, but that is far from being all day long; and you would choose your time very ill if you applied to a man about one business when his head was full of another, or when his heart was full of grief, anger, or any other disagreeable sentiment.

JUDGE OF OTHER MEN'S FEELINGS BY YOUR OWN.— In order to judge of the inside of others, study your own; for men, in general, are very much alike; and though one has one prevailing passion, and another has another, yet their operations are much the same; and whatever engages or disgusts, pleases or offends you, in others, will, *mutatis mutandis*, engage, disgust, please, or offend others in you. Observe, with the utmost attention, all the operations of your own mind, the nature of your passions, and the various motives that determine your will; and you may, in a great degree, know all mankind. For instance: do you find yourself hurt and mortified when another makes you feel his superiority and your own inferiority in knowledge, parts, rank, or fortune? you will certainly take great care not to make a person, whose good will, good word, interest, esteem, or friendship, you would gain, feel that superiority in you, in case you have it. Disagreeable insinuations, sly sneers, or repeated contradictions, tease and irritate you, would you use them where you wished to engage and please? Surely not; and I hope you wish to engage and please almost universally. The temptation of saying a smart and witty thing, or *bon mot*, and the malicious applause with which it is commonly received, have made people who can say them, and, still oftener, people who think they can, but cannot, and yet try. more enemies, and implacable ones too, than any one other thing that I know of. When such things, then, shall happen to be said at your expense (as sometimes they certainly will), reflect seriously upon the sentiments of uneasiness, anger, and resentment, which they excite in you; and consider whether it can be prudent, by the same means, to excite the same sentiments in others against you. It is a decided folly to lose a friend for a jest; but, in my mind, it is not a much less degree of folly to make an enemy of an indifferent and neutral person for the sake of a *bon mot*. When things of this kind happen to be said of you, the most prudent way is to seem not to suppose that they are meant at you, but to dissemble and conceal whatever degree of anger you may feel inwardly; and, should they be so plain that you cannot be supposed ignorant of their meaning, to join in the laugh of the company against yourself, acknowledge the hit to be a fair one, and the jest a good one, and play off the whole thing in seeming good humour: but by no means reply in the same way; which only shews that you are hurt, and publishes the victory which you might have concealed. Should the thing said, indeed, injure your honour or moral character, remember there are but two alternatives for a gentleman and a man of parts —extreme politeness or a duel.

AVOID SEEING AN AFFRONT, IF POSSIBLE.—If a man notoriously and designedly insults and affronts you, knock him down; but if he only injures you, your best revenge is to be extremely civil to him in your outward behaviour, though, at the same time, you counterwork him, and return him the compliment perhaps, with interest. This is not perfidy nor dissimulation ; it would be so, if you were, at the same time, to make professions of esteem and friendship to this man ; which I by no means recommend, but, on the contrary, abhor. All acts of civility are, by common consent, understood to be no more than a conformity to custom, for the quiet and conveniency of society, the *agrémens* of which are not to be disturbed by private dislikes and jealousies. Only women and little minds pout and spar for the entertainment of the company, that always laugh at and never pity them. For my own part, though I would by no means give up any point to a competitor, yet I would pique myself upon shewing him rather more civility than to another man. In the first place, this behaviour infallibly makes all the laughers on your side, which is a considerable party ; and, in the next place, it certainly pleases the object of the competition, be it either man or woman ; who never fail to say, upon such an occasion, that ' they must own you have behaved yourself very handsomely in the whole affair.'

DISSEMBLE RESENTMENT TOWARDS ENEMIES. — In short, let this be one invariable rule of your conduct : Never to shew the least symptom of resentment which you cannot, to a certain degree, gratify ; but always to smile when you cannot strike. There would be no living in the world if one could not conceal and even dissemble the just causes of resentment, which one meets with every day in active and busy life. Whoever cannot master his humour should leave the world, and retire to some hermitage in an unfrequented desert. By shewing an unavailing and sullen resentment, you authorise the resentment of those who can hurt you, and whom you cannot hurt ; and give them that very pretence which, perhaps, they wished for, of breaking with and injuring you ; whereas the contrary behaviour would lay them under the restraints of decency, at least, and either shackle or expose their malice. Besides, captiousness, sullenness, and pouting are most exceedingly illiberal and vulgar.

TRUST NOT TOO MUCH TO ANY MAN'S HONESTY.— Though men are all of one composition, the several ingredients are so differently proportioned in each individual that no two are exactly alike ; and no one, at all times, like himself. The ablest man will, some-times, do weak things ; the proudest man mean things ; the honestest man ill things ; and the wickedest man good things. Study individuals then ; and, if you take (as you ought to do) their outlines from their prevailing passion, suspend your last finishing strokes till you have attended to and discovered the operations of their inferior passions, appetites, and humours. A man's general character may be that of the honestest man in the world : do not dispute it ; you might be thought envious or ill-natured ; but, at the same time, do not take this probity upon trust to such a degree as to put your life, fortune, or reputation, in his power. This honest man may happen to be your rival in power, in interest, or in love ; three passions that often put honesty to most severe trials, in which it is too often cast ; but first analyze this honest man yourself, and then only you will be able to judge how far you may or may not with safety trust him.

STUDY THE FOIBLES AND PASSIONS OF BOTH SEXES. —If you would particularly gain the affection and friendship of particular people, whether man or woman, endeavour to find out their predominant excellency, if they have one, and their prevailing weakness, which every body has ; and do justice to the one, and something more than justice to the other. Men have various objects in which they may excel, or, at least, would be thought to excel ; and, though they love to hear justice done to them where they know that they excel, yet they are most and best flattered upon those points where they wish to excel, and yet are doubtful whether they do or not. As, for example : Cardinal Richelieu, who was undoubtedly the ablest statesman of his time, or perhaps of any other, had the idle vanity of being thought the best poet too ; he envied the great Corneille his reputation, and

ordered a criticism to be written on the *Cid*. Those,
therefore, who flattered skilfully said little to him of
his abilities in state affairs, or, at least, but *en passant*,
and as it might naturally occur. But the incense
which they gave him, the smoke of which they knew
would turn his head in their favour, was as a *bel
esprit* and a poet. Why? because he was sure of
one excellency, and distrustful as to the other.

FLATTER THE VANITY OF ALL.—You will easily
discover every man's prevailing vanity, by observing
his favourite topic or conversation; for every man
talks most of what he has most a mind to be thought
to excel in. Touch him but there, and you touch
him to the quick.

Women have in general but one object, which is
their beauty; upon which scarce any flattery is too
gross for them to swallow. Nature has hardly formed
a woman ugly enough to be insensible to flattery
upon her person. If her face is so shocking that she
must, in some degree, be conscious of it, her figure
and her air, she trusts, make ample amends for it.
If her figure is deformed, her face, she thinks, coun-
terbalances it. If they are both bad, she comforts
herself that she has graces, a certain manner, a *je ne
sais quoi*, still more engaging than beauty. This truth
is evident, from the studied and elaborate dress of the
ugliest women in the world. An undoubted, uncon-
tested, conscious beauty is, of all women, the least
sensible of flattery upon that head; she knows it is
her due, and is therefore obliged to nobody for giving
it her. She must be flattered upon her understanding; which, though she may possibly not doubt of
herself, yet she suspects that men may distrust.

Do not mistake me, and think that I mean to
recommend to you abject and criminal flattery; no:
flatter nobody's vices nor crimes; on the contrary,
abhor and discourage them. But there is no living
in the world without a complaisant indulgence for
people's weaknesses and innocent though ridiculous
vanities. If a man has a mind to be thought wiser
and a woman handsomer than they really are, their

error is a comfortable one to themselves, and an innocent one with regard to other people; and I would rather make them my friends, by indulging them in it, than my enemies, by endeavouring (and that to no purpose) to undeceive them.

SUSPECT THOSE WHO REMARKABLY AFFECT ANY ONE VIRTUE.— Suspect, in general, those who remarkably affect any one virtue; who raise it above all others, and who, in a manner, intimate that they possess it exclusively: I say, suspect them; for they are commonly impostors: but do not be sure that they are always so; for I have sometimes known saints really religious, blusterers really brave, reformers of mankind really honest, and prudes really chaste. Pry into the recesses of their hearts yourself, as far as you are able, and never implicitly adopt a character upon common fame, which, though generally right as to great outlines of characters, is always wrong in some particulars.

GUARD AGAINST PROFFERED FRIENDSHIP.—Be upon your guard against those who, upon very slight acquaintance, obtrude their unasked and unmerited friendship and confidence upon you; for they probably cram you with them only for their own eating; but, at the same time, do not roughly reject them upon that general supposition. Examine farther, and see whether those unexpected offers flow from a warm heart and a silly head, or from a designing head and a cold heart; for knavery and folly have often the same symptoms. In the first case, there is no danger in accepting them—*valeant quantum valere possunt.* In the latter case, it may be useful to seem to accept them, and artfully to turn the battery upon him who raised it.

DISBELIEVE ASSERTIONS BY OATHS.—If a man uses strong oaths or protestations to make you believe a thing which is of itself so likely and probable that the bare saying of it would be sufficient, depend upon it he lies, and is highly interested in making you believe it; or else he would not take so much pains

Shun riotous connexions.—There is an incontinency of friendship among young fellows, who are associated by their mutual pleasures only, which has, very frequently, bad consequences. A parcel of warm hearts and unexperienced heads, heated with convivial mirth, and possibly a little too much wine, vow, and really mean at the time, eternal friendships to each other, and indiscreetly pour out their whole souls in common, and without the least reserve. These confidences are as indiscreetly repealed as they were made; for new pleasures and new places soon dissolve this ill-cemented connexion, and then very ill uses are made of these rash confidences. Bear your part, however, in young companies; nay, excel, if you can, in all the social and convivial joy and festivity that become youth. Trust them with your love tales, if you please; but keep your serious views secret. Trust those only to some tried friend, more experienced than yourself, and who, being in a different walk of life from you, is not likely to become your rival; for I would not advise you to depend so much upon the heroic virtue of mankind as to hope or believe that your competitor will ever be your friend, as to the object of that competition.

A seeming ignorance often necessary.—A seeming ignorance is often a most necessary part of worldly knowledge. It is, for instance, commonly advisable to seem ignorant of what people offer to tell you; and, when they say, Have you not heard of such a thing? to answer, No: and to let them go on, though you know it already. Some have a pleasure in telling it, because they think they tell it well; others have a pride in it, as being the sagacious discoverers; and many have a vanity in shewing that they have been, though very undeservedly, trusted; all these would be disappointed, and consequently displeased, if you said, Yes. Seem always ignorant (unless to one most intimate friend) of all matters of private scandal and defamation, though you should hear them a thousand times; for the parties affected always look upon the receiver to be almost as bad as the thief; and, whenever they become the topic of conversation, seem to be a sceptic, though you are really a serious believer; and always take the extenu-ating part. But all this seeming ignorance should be joined to thorough and extensive private information; and, indeed, it is the best method of procuring them; for most people have such a vanity in shewing a superiority over others, though but for a moment, and in the merest trifles, that they will tell you what they should not, rather than not shew that they can tell what you did not know; besides that such seeming ignorance will make you pass for incurious, and con-sequently undesigning. However, fish for facts, and take pains to be well informed of every thing that passes; but fish judiciously, and not always, nor in-deed often, in the shape of direct questions, which always put people on their guard, and, often repeated, grow tiresome. But, sometimes, take the things that you would know for granted; upon which somebody will, kindly and officiously, set you right: sometimes say that you have heard so and so; and, at other times, seem to know more than you do, in order to know all that you want: but avoid direct questioning as much as you can.

FLEXIBILITY OF MANNERS VERY USEFUL.—Human nature is the same all over the world, but its opera-tions are so varied by education and habit that one must see it in all its dresses, in order to be intimately acquainted with it. The passion of ambition, for instance, is the same in a courtier, a soldier, or an ecclesiastic; but, from their different educations and habits, they will take very different methods to gratify it. Civility, which is a disposition to accommodate and oblige others, is essentially the same in every country; but good breeding, as it is called, which is the manner of exerting that disposition, is different in almost every country, and merely local; and every man of sense imitates and conforms to that local good breeding of the place where he is at. A con-formity and flexibility of manners is necessary in the course of the world; that is, with regard to all things which are not wrong in themselves. The *versatile ingenium* is the most useful of all. It can turn itself instantly from one object to another, assuming the proper manner for each. It can be serious with the grave, cheerful with the gay, and trifling with the frivolous.

Indeed, nothing is more engaging than a cheerful and easy conformity to people's particular manners, habits, and even weaknesses; nothing (to use a vulgar expression) should come amiss to a young fellow. He should be, for good purposes, what Alcibiades was commonly for bad ones,—a Proteus, assuming with ease, and wearing with cheerfulness, any shape. Heat, cold, luxury, abstinence, gravity, gaiety, ceremony, easiness, learning, trifling, business, and pleasure, are modes which he should be able to take, lay aside, or change occasionally, with as much ease as he would take or lay aside his hat.

SPIRIT.—Young men are apt to think that every thing is to be carried by spirit and vigour; that art is meanness, and versatility and complaisance are the refuge of pusillanimity and weakness. This most mistaken opinion gives an indelicacy, an abruptness, and a roughness, to the manners. Fools, who can never be undeceived, retain them as long as they live; reflection, with a little experience, makes men of sense shake them off soon. When they come to be a little better acquainted with themselves, and with their own species, they discover, that plain, right reason is, nine times in ten, the fettered and shackled attendant of the triumph of the heart and the passions; consequently, they address themselves nine times in ten to the conqueror; not to the conquered: and conquerors, you know, must be applied to in the gentlest, the most engaging, and the most insinuating manner.

But, unfortunately, young men are as apt to think themselves wise enough, as drunken men are to think themselves sober enough. They look upon spirit to be a much better thing than experience; which they call coldness. They are but half mistaken; for, though spirit without experience is dangerous, experience without spirit is languid and defective. Their union, which is very rare, is perfection; you may join them, if you please; for all my experience is at your service; and I do not desire one grain of your spirit in return. Use them both, and let them reciprocally animate and check each other. I mean here, by the spirit of youth, only the vivacity and presumption of youth, which hinder them from seeing the difficulties or dangers of an undertaking: but I do not mean what the silly vulgar call spirit, by which they are captious, jealous of their rank, suspicious of being undervalued, and tart (as they call it) in their repartees upon the slightest occasions. This is an evil and a very silly spirit, which should be driven out, and transferred to a herd of swine.

NEVER NEGLECT OLD ACQUAINTANCE.—To conclude; never neglect or despise old, for the sake of new or shining, acquaintance; which would be ungrateful on your part, and never forgiven on theirs. Take care to make as many personal friends, and as few personal enemies, as possible. I do not mean, by personal friends, intimate and confidential friends, of which no man can hope to have half a dozen in the whole course of his life; but I mean friends, in the common acceptation of the word; that is, people who speak well of you, and who would rather do you good than harm, consistently with their own interest, and no farther.

LYING.

NOTHING is more criminal, mean, or ridiculous, than lying. It is the production either of malice, cowardice, or vanity; but it generally misses of its aim in every one of these views; for lies are always detected sooner or later. If we advance a malicious lie, in order to affect any man's fortune or character, we may, indeed, injure him for some time; but we shall certainly be the greatest sufferers in the er for, as soon as we are detected, we are blasted for the infamous attempt; and, whatever is said afterward to the disadvantage of that person, however true, passes for calumny. To lie, or to equivocate (which is the same thing), to excuse ourselves for what we have said or done, and to avoid the danger or the shame that we apprehend from it, we discover our fear as well as our falsehood; and only increase, instead of avoiding, the danger and the shame; we shew ourselves to be the lowest and meanest of mankind, and are sure to be always treated as such. If we have the misfortune to be in the wrong, there is something noble in frankly owning it; it is the only way of atoning for it, and the only way to be forgiven. To remove a present danger, by equivocating, evading, or shuffling, is something so despicable, and betrays so much fear, that whoever practises it deserves to be chastised.

There are people who indulge themselves in another sort of lying, which they reckon innocent, and which, in one sense, is so; for it hurts nobody but themselves. This sort of lying is the spurious offspring of vanity begotten upon folly. These people deal in the marvellous. They have seen some things that never existed; they have seen other things which they never really saw, though they did exist, only because they were thought worth seeing. Has any thing remarkable been said or done in any place, or in any company, they immediately represent and declare themselves eye or ear witnesses of it. They have done feats themselves, unattempted, or at least unperformed, by others. They are always the heroes of their own fables; and think that they gain consideration, or at least present attention, by it. Whereas, in truth, all that they get is ridicule and contempt, not without a good degree of distrust: for, one must naturally conclude, that he, who will tell any lie from idle vanity, will not scruple telling a greater for interest. Had I really seen any thing so very extraordinary as to be almost incredible, I would keep it to myself, rather than, by telling it, give any body room to doubt for one minute of my veracity. It is most certain, that the reputation of chastity is not so necessary for a woman, as that of veracity is for a man, and with reason; for it is possible for a woman to be virtuous though not strictly chaste: but it is not possible for a man to be virtuous without strict veracity. The slips of the poor woman are sometimes mere bodily frailties; but a lie in a man is a vice in the mind and of the heart.

Nothing but truth can carry us through the world with either our conscience or our honour unwounded. It is not only our duty, but our interest: as a proof of which it may be observed, that the greatest fools are the greatest liars. We may safely judge by a man's truth of his degree of understanding.

DIGNITY OF MANNERS.

A CERTAIN dignity of manners is absolutely necessary, to make even the most valuable characters either respected or respectable in the world.

ROMPING, &c.—Horseplay, romping, frequent and loud fits of laughter, jokes, waggery, and indiscriminate familiarity, will sink both merit and knowledge into a degree of contempt. They compose at most a merry fellow, and a merry fellow was never yet a respectable man. Indiscriminate familiarity either offends your superiors, or else dubs you their dependant and led captain. It gives your inferiors just but troublesome and improper claims of equality. A joker is near akin to a buffoon; and neither of them is the least related to wit. Whoever is admitted or sought for, in company, upon any other account than that of his merit and manners, is never respected there, but only made use of. We will have Such-a-one, for he sings prettily; We will invite Such-a-one to a ball, for he dances well; We will have Such-a-one to supper, for he is always joking and laughing; We will ask another, because he plays deep at all games, or because he can drink a great deal. These are all vilifying distinctions, mortifying preferences and exclude all ideas of esteem and regard. Whoever is had (as it is called) in company, for the sake of any one thing singly, is singly that thing, and will never be considered in any other light; and consequently never respected, let his merits be what they will.

PRIDE.—Dignity of manners is not only as different from pride as true courage is from blustering, or true wit from joking, but is absolutely inconsistent with it; for nothing vilifies and degrades more than pride. The pretensions of the proud man are oftener treated with sneer and contempt than with indignation, as we offer ridiculously too little to a tradesman who asks ridiculously too much for his goods; but we do not haggle with one who only asks a just and reasonable price.

ABJECT FLATTERY.—Abject flattery and indiscriminate ostentation degrade, as much as indiscriminate contradiction and noisy debate disgust; but a modest assertion of one's own opinion, and a complaisant acquiescence to other people's preserve dignity.

Vulgar, low expressions, awkward notions and address, vilify, as they imply either a very low turn of mind, or low education and low company.

FRIVOLOUS CURIOSITY.—Frivolous curiosity about trifles, and a laborious attention to little objects, which neither require nor deserve a moment's thought, lower a man: who thence is thought (and not unjustly) incapable of greater matters. Cardinal de Retz very sagaciously marked out Cardinal Chigi for a little mind, from the moment that he told him he had written three years with the same pen, and that it was an excellent good one still.

A certain degree of exterior seriousness in looks and motions gives dignity, without excluding wit and decent cheerfulness, which are always serious themselves. A constant smirk upon the face, and a whiffling activity of the body, are strong indications of futility. Whoever is in a hurry, shews that the thing he is about is too big for him. Haste and hurry are very different things.

To conclude: a man who has patiently been kick-
ed, may as well pretend to courage, as a man, blasted
by vices and crimes, may to dignity of any kind. But
an exterior decency and dignity of manners will even
keep such a man longer from sinking than otherwise
he would be; of such consequence is *decorum*, even
though affected and put on.

GENTLENESS OF MANNERS,

WITH FIRMNESS OR RESOLUTION OF MIND.

I DO not know any one rule so unexceptionably useful
and necessary, in every part of life, as to unite *gentleness of manners with firmness of mind*. The first
alone would degenerate and sink into a mean, timid
complaisance, and passiveness, if not supported and
dignified by the latter; which would also deviate into
impetuosity and brutality, if not tempered and softened
by the other; however, they are seldom united. The
warm, choleric man, with strong animal spirits, de-
spises the first, and thinks to carry all before him by
the last. He may, possibly, by great accident, now
and then succeed, when he has only weak and timid
people to deal with; but his general fate will be to
shock, offend, be hated, and fail. On the other hand,
the cunning, crafty man thinks to gain all his ends by
gentleness of manners only; *he becomes all things to
all men;* he seems to have no opinion of his own, and
servilely adopts the present opinion of the present
person: he insinuates himself only into the esteem of
fools, but is soon detected and surely despised by every
body else. The wise man (who differs as much from
the cunning as from the choleric man) alone joins
softness of manners with firmness of mind.

DELIVER COMMANDS WITH MILDNESS.—The advantages arising from a union of these qualities are equally
striking and obvious. For example: if you are in
authority, and have a right to command, your commands delivered with mildness and gentleness will be
willingly, cheerfully, and consequently well obeyed;

whereas, if given brutally, they will rather be interpreted than executed. For, a cool, steady resolution shoudl shew, that where you have a right to command you will be obeyed ; but, at the same time, a gentleness in the manner of enforcing that obedience should make it a cheerful one, and soften, as much as possible, the mortifying consciousness of inferiority.

ASK A FAVOUR WITH SOFTNESS.—If you are to ask a favour, or even to solicit your due, you must do it with a grace, or you will give those who have a mind to refuse you a pretence to do it, by resenting the manner ; but, on the other hand, you must, by a steady perseverance and decent tenaciousness, shew firmness and resolution. The right motives are seldom the true ones of men's actions, especially of people in high stations : who often give to importunity and fear what they would refuse to justice or to merit. By gentleness and softness engage their hearts, if you can ; at least, prevent the pretence of offence ; but take care to shew resolution and firmness enough to extort from their love of ease or their fear what you might in vain hope for from their justice or good-nature. People in high life are hardened to the wants and distresses of mankind, as surgeons are to their bodily pains : they see and hear them all day long, and even of so many simulated ones, that they do not know which are real and which are not. Other sentiments are therefore to be applied to than those of mere justice and humanity. Their favour must be captivated by the graces, their love of ease disturbed by unwearied importunity, or their fear wrought upon by a decent intimation of implacable cool resentment. This precept is the only way I know in the world of being loved without being despised, and feared without being hated. It constitutes the dignity of character which every wise man must endeavour to establish.

CHECK HASTINESS OF TEMPER.—To conclude : If you find that you have a hastiness in your temper, which unguardedly breaks out into indiscreet sallies, or rough expressions to either your superiors, your equals, or your inferiors, watch it narrowly, check it carefully, and call the graces to your assistance. At the first impulse of passion, be silent, till you can be soft. Labour even to get the command of your countenance so well that those emotions may not be read in it : a most unspeakable advantage in business! On the other hand, let no complaisance, no gentleness of temper, no weak desire of pleasing, on your part, —no wheedling, coaxing, nor flattery, on other people's—make you recede one jot from any point that reason and justice have bid you pursue ; but return to the charge, persist, persevere, and you will find most things attainable that are possible. A yielding, timid meekness is always abused and insulted by the unjust and the unfeeling ; but, when sustained by firmness and resolution, is always respected, commonly successful.

In your friendships and connexions, as well as in your enmities, this rule is particularly useful ; let your firmness and vigour preserve and invite attachments to you ; but, at the same time, let your manner hinder the enemies of your friends and dependants from becoming yours : let your enemies be disarmed by the gentleness of your manner, but let them feel, at the same time, the steadiness of your just resentment ; for there is great difference between bearing malice, which is always ungenerous, and a resolute self-defence, which is always prudent and justifiable.

BE CIVIL, &c. TO RIVALS OR COMPETITORS.—Some people cannot gain upon themselves to be easy and civil to those who are either their rivals, competitors, or opposers, though, independently of those accidental circumstances, they would like and esteem them. They betray a shyness and awkwardness in company with them, and catch at any little thing to expose them ; and so, from temporary and only occasional opponents, make them their personal enemies. This is exceedingly weak and detrimental, as, indeed, is all humour in business ; which can only be carried on successfully by unadulterated good policy and right reasoning. In such situations I would be more particularly civil, easy, and frank with the man whose designs I traversed; this is commonly called generosity and magnanimity, but is, in truth, good sense and policy. The manner is often as important as the matter; sometimes more so: a favour may make an enemy, and an injury may make a friend, according to the different manner in which they are severally done. In fine, gentleness of manners, with firmness of mind, is a short but full description of human perfections on this side of religious and moral duties.

MORAL CHARACTER.

THE moral character of a man should be not only pure, but, like Cæsar's wife, unsuspected. The least speck or blemish upon it is fatal. Nothing degrades and vilifies more; for it excites and unites detestation and contempt. There are, however, wretches in the world profligate enough to explode all notions of moral good and evil; to maintain that they are merely local, and depend entirely upon the customs and fashions of different countries: nay, there are still, if possible, more unaccountable wretches; I mean, those who affect to preach and propagate such absurd and infamous notions, without believing them themselves. Avoid, as much as possible, the company of such people, who reflect a degree of discredit and infamy upon all who converse with them. But, as you may sometimes, by accident, fall into such company, take great care that no complaisance, no good humour, no warmth of festal mirth, ever make you seem to acquiesce in, much less approve or applaud, such infamous doctrines. On the other hand, do not debate, nor enter into serious argument, upon a subject so much below it: but content yourself with telling them, that you know they are not serious; that you have a much better opinion of them than they would have you have; and that you are very sure they would not practise the doctrine they preach. But put your private mark upon them, and shun them for ever afterward.

There is nothing so delicate as a man's moral character, and nothing which it is his interest so much to preserve pure. Should he be suspected of injustice, malignity, perfidy, lying, &c., all the parts and knowledge in the world will never procure him esteem, friendship, or respect. I therefore recommend to you a most scrupulous tenderness for your moral character, and the utmost care not to say or do the least thing that may, ever so slightly, taint it. Shew yourself, upon all occasions, the friend, but not the bully, of virtue. Even Colonel Chartres (who was the most notorious rascal in the world, and who had, by all sorts of crimes, amassed immense wealth), sensible of the disadvantage of a bad character, was once heard to say, that 'although he would not give one farthing for virtue, he would give ten thousand pounds for a character; because he should get a hundred thousand pounds by it.' Is it possible, then, that an honest man can neglect what a wise rogue would purchase so dear?

There is one of the vices above-mentioned, into which people of good education, and, in the main, of good principles, sometimes fall, from mistaken notions of skill, dexterity, and self-defence; I mean lying; though it is inseparably attended with more infamy and loss than any other. But I have before given you my sentiments very freely on this subject; I shall therefore conclude this head with entreating you to be scrupulously jealous of the purity of your moral character; keep it immaculate, unblemished, unsullied, and it will be unsuspected. Defamation and calumny never attack where there is no weak place; they magnify, but they do not create.

COMMONPLACE OBSERVATIONS.

NEVER use, believe, or approve commonplace observations. They are the common topics of witlin s and coxcombs; those who really have wit have the utmost contempt for them, and scorn even to laugh at the pert things that those would-be wits say upon such subjects.

RELIGION.—Religion is one of their favourite topics; it is all priestcraft, and an invention contrived and carried on by priests of all religions, for their own power and profit. From this absurd and false principle flow the commonplace and insipid jokes and insults upon the clergy. With these people, every priest of every religion is either a public or a concealed unbeliever, drunkard, and whoremaster; whereas, I conceive, that priests are extremely like other men, and neither the better nor the worse for wearing a gown or a surplice; but, if they are different from other people, probably it is rather on the side of religion and morality, or at least decency, from their education and manner of life.

MATRIMONY.—Another common topic for false wit and cold raillery is matrimony. Every man and his wife hate each other cordially, whatever they may pretend, in public, to the contrary. The husband certainly wishes his wife at the devil, and the wife certainly cuckolds her husband. Whereas, I presume, that men and their wives neither love nor hate each other the more, upon account of the form of matrimony which has been said over them. The cohabitation, indeed, which is the consequence of matrimony, makes them either love or hate more, accordingly as they respectively deserve it; but that would be exactly the same between any man and woman who lived together without being married.

COURTS AND COTTAGES.—It is also a trite commonplace observation, that courts are the seats of falsehood and dissimulation. That, like many, I might say most, commonplace observations, is false. Falsehood and dissimulation are certainly to be found at courts; but where are they not to be found? Cottages have them as well as courts, only with worse manners. A couple of neighbouring farmers in a village will contrive and practise as many tricks to overreach each other at the next market, or to supplant each other in the favour of the squire, as any two courtiers can do to supplant each other in the favour of their prince. Whatever poets may write, or fools believe, of rural innocence and truth, and of the perfidy of courts, this is undoubtedly true,—that shepherds and ministers are both men; their natute and passions the same; the modes of them only different.

These and many other commonplace reflections upon nations or professions, in general (which are at least as often false as true), are the poor refuge of people who have neither wit nor invention of their own, but endeavour to shine in company by second-hand finery. I always put these pert jackanapes out of countenance, by looking extremely grave when they expect that I should laugh at their pleasantries ; and by saying, *Well, and so?* as if they had not done, and that the sting were still to come. This disconcerts them ; as they have no resources in themselves, and have but one set of jokes to live upon. Men of parts are not reduced to these shifts, and have the utmost contempt for them ; they find proper subjects enough for either useful or lively conversation ; they can be witty without satire or commonplace, and serious without being dull.

ORATORY.

ORATORY, or the art of speaking well, is useful in every situation of life, and absolutely necessary in most. A man cannot distinguish himself without it. in parliament, in the pulpit, or at the bar ; and even in common conversation, he who has acquired an easy and habitual eloquence, and who speaks with propriety and accuracy, will have a great advantage over those who speak inelegantly and incorrectly. The business of oratory is to persuade, and to please is the most effectual step towards persuading. It is very advantageous for a man who speaks in public to please his hearers so much as to gain their attention, which he cannot possibly do without the assistance of oratory.

It is certain, that by study and application every man may make himself a tolerably good orator, eloquence depending upon observation and care. Every man may, if he please, make choice of good instead of bad words and phrases, may speak with propriety instead of impropriety, and may be clear and perspicuous in his recitals, instead of dark and unintelligible; he may have grace instead of awkwardness in his gestures and deportment; in short, it is in the power of every man, with pains and application, to be a very agreeable, instead of a very disagreeable speaker; and it is well worth the labour to excel other men in that particular article in which they excel beasts.

Demosthenes thought it so essentially necessary to speak well, that, though he naturally stuttered, and had weak lungs, he resolved, by application, to overcome these disadvantages. He cured his stammering by putting small pebbles into his mouth; and gradually strengthened his lungs, by daily using himself to speak loudly and distinctly for a considerable time. In stormy weather he often visited the sea-shore, where he spoke as loud as he could, in order to prepare himself for the noise and murmurs of the popular assemblies of the Athenians, before whom he was to speak. By this extraordinary care and attention, and the constant study of the best authors, he became the greatest orator that his own or any other age or country has produced.

Whatever language a person uses, he should speak it in its greatest purity, and according to the rules of grammar; nor is it sufficient that we do not speak a language ill, we must endeavour to speak it well: for which purpose, we should read the best authors with attention, and observe how people of fashion and education speak. Common people, in general, speak ill; they make use of inelegant and vulgar expressions, which people of rank never do. In numbers they frequently join the singular and plural together, and seldom make choice of the proper tense. To avoid all these faults, we should read with attention, and observe the turn and expressions of the best authors ; nor should we pass over a word we do not perfectly understand, without searching and inquiring for the exact meaning of it.

It is said that a man must be born a poet, but it is in his power to make himself an orator ; for to be a poet requires a certain degree of strength and vivacity of mind ; but that attention, reading, and labour are sufficient to form an orator.

PEDANTRY.

EVERY excellence, and every virtue, has its kindred vice or weakness ; and, if carried beyond certain bounds, sinks into the one or the other. Generosity often runs into profusion, economy into avarice, courage into rashness, caution into timidity, and so on ;—insomuch that, I believe, there is more judgment required for the proper conduct of our virtues than for avoiding their opposite vices. Vice, in its true light, is so deformed that it shocks at first sight ; and would hardly ever seduce us, if it did not, at first, wear the mask of some virtue. But virtue is, in itself, so beautiful, that it charms us at first sight ; engages us more and more upon farther acquaintance ; and, as with other beauties, we think excess impossible : it is here that judgment is necessary to moderate and direct the efforts of an excellent cause. In the same manner, great learning, if not accompanied with sound judgment, frequently carries us into error, pride, and pedantry.

NEVER PRONOUNCE ARBITRARILY.—Some learned men, proud of their knowledge, only speak to decide, and give judgment without appeal ; the consequence of which is, that mankind, provoked by the insult, and injured by the oppression, revolt : and, in order to shake off the tyranny, even call the lawful authority in question. The more you know, the modester you should be; and that modesty is the surest way of gratifying your vanity. Even where you are sure, seem rather doubtful; represent, but do not pronounce; and, if you would convince others, seem open to conviction yourself.

AFFECT NOT TO PREFER THE ANCIENTS TO THE MODERNS.—Others, to shew their learning, or often from the prejudices of a school education, where they hear of nothing else, are always talking of the ancients as something more than men, and of the moderns as something less. They are never without a classic or two in their pockets; they stick to the old good sense; they read none of the modern trash; and will shew you plainly, that no improvement has been made, in any one art or science, these last seventeen hundred years. I would by no means have you disown your acquaintance with the ancients; but still less would I have you brag of an exclusive intimacy with them. Speak of the moderns without contempt, and of the ancients without idolatry; judge them all by their merits, but not by their ages: and, if you happen to have an Elzevir classic in your pocket, neither shew it nor mention it.

REASON NOT FROM ANCIENT AUTHENTICITY.—Some great scholars, most absurdly, draw all their maxims, both for public and private life, from what they call parallel cases in the ancient authors; without considering that, in the first place, there never were, since the creation of the world, two cases exactly parallel; and, in the next place, that there never was a case stated, or even known, by any historian, with every one of its circumstances; which, however, ought to be known, in order to be reasoned from. Reason upon the case itself, and the several circumstances that attend it, and act accordingly; but not from the authority of ancient poets or historians. Take into your consideration, if you please, cases seemingly analogous; but take them as helps only, not as guides.

ABSTAIN FROM LEARNED OSTENTATION.—There is another species of learned men, who, though less dogmatical and supercilious, are not less impertinent. These are the communicative and shining pedants, who adorn their conversation, even with women, by happy quotations of Greek and Latin, and who have contracted such a familiarity with the Greek and Roman authors, that they call them by certain names or epithets, denoting intimacy; as *old* Homer; that *sly rogue* Horace; *Maro*, instead of Virgil; *Naso*, instead of Ovid. These are often imitated by coxcombs who have no learning at all; but who have got some names and some scraps of ancient authors by heart, which they improperly and impertinently retail in all companies, in hopes of passing for scholars. If, therefore, you would avoid the accusation of pedantry on one hand, or the suspicion of ignorance on the other, abstain from learned ostentation. Speak the language of the company you are in; speak it purely, and un-larded with any other. Nor seem wiser nor more learned than the people you are with. Wear your learning like your watch, in a private pocket; and do not pull it out and strike it, merely to show that you have one. If you are asked what o'clock it is, tell it; but do not proclaim it hourly and unasked, like the watchman.

PLEASURE.

MANY young people adopt pleasures for which they have not the least taste, only because they are called by that name. They often mistake so totally as to imagine that debauchery is pleasure. Drunkenness, which is equally destructive to body and mind, is certainly a fine pleasure! Gaming, which draws us into a thousand scrapes, leaves us pennyless, and gives us the air and manners of an outrageous mad-man, is another most exquisite pleasure!

Pleasure is the rock which most young people split upon; they launch out with crowded sails in quest of it, but without a compass to direct their course, or reason sufficient to steer the vessel; therefore pain and shame, instead of pleasure, are the returns of their voyage.

A man of pleasure, in the vulgar acceptation of that phrase, means only a beastly drunkard, an abandoned rake, and profligate swearer; we should weigh the present enjoyment of our pleasures against the unavoidable consequences of them, and then let our common sense determine the choice.

We may enjoy the pleasures of the table and the wine, but stop short of the pains inseparably annexed to an excess in either. We may let other people do as they will, without formally and sententiously rebuking them for it; but we must be firmly resolved not to destroy our own faculties and constitution, in compliance to those who have no regard to their own. We may play to give us pleasure, but not to give us pain; we may play for trifles in mixed companies, to amuse ourselves, and conform to custom. Good company are not fond of having a man reeling drunk among them; nor is it agreeable to see another tearing his hair and blaspheming, for having lost, at play, more than he is able to pay; or a rake, with half a nose, crippled by coarse and infamous debauches. Those who practise and brag of these things make no part of good company; and are most unwillingly, if ever, admitted into it. A real man of fashion and pleasure observes decency; at least he neither borrows nor affects vices: and if he is so unfortunate as to have any, he gratifies them with choice, delicacy, and secrecy.

We should be as attentive to our pleasures as to our studies. In the latter we should observe and reflect upon all we read; and in the former, be watchful and attentive to every thing we see and hear: and let us never have it to say, as some fools do, of things that were said and done before their faces, 'That indeed they did not mind them, because they were thinking of something else.' Why were they thinking of something else? And if they were, why did they come there? Wherever we are we should (as it is vulgarly expressed) have our ears and our eyes about us. We should listen to every thing that is said, and see every thing that is done. Let us observe, without being thought overseers; for, otherwise people will be upon their guard before us.

All gaming, field sports, and such other amusements, where neither the understanding nor the senses have the least share, are frivolous, and the resources of little minds who either do not think or do not love to think. But the pleasures of a man of parts either flatter the senses or improve the mind.

There are liberal and illiberal pleasures, as well as liberal and illiberal arts. Sottish drunkenness, indiscriminate gluttony, driving coaches, rustic sports, such as fox-chases, horse-races, &c. are infinitely below the honest and industrious professions of a tailor and a shoemaker.

The more we apply to business, the more we relish our pleasures; the exercise of the mind in the morning, by study, whets the appetite for the pleasures of the evening, as the exercise of the body whets the appetite for dinner. Business and pleasure, rightly understood, mutually assist each other, — instead of being enemies, as foolish or dull people often think them. We cannot taste pleasures truly, unless we earn them by previous business; and few people do business well, who do nothing else. But, when I speak of pleasures, I always mean the elegant pleasures of a rational being, and not the brutal ones of a swine.

PREJUDICES.

NEVER adopt the notions of any books you may read, or of any company you may keep, without examining whether they are just or not; as you will otherwise be liable to be hurried away by prejudices, instead of being guided by reason, and quietly cherish error, instead of seeking for truth.

Use and assert your own reason; reflect, examine,

and analyze every thing, in order to form a sound and mature judgment; let no *ipse dixit* impose upon your understanding, mislead your actions, dictate your conversation. Be early, what, if you are not, you will, when too late, wish you had been. Consult your reason betimes, I do not say that it will always prove an unerring guide, for human reason is not infallible; but it will prove the least erring guide that you can follow. Books and conversation may assist it, but adopt neither blindly and implicitly; try both by that best rule, which God has given to direct us,— reason. Of all the troubles, do not decline, as many people do, that of thinking. The herd of mankind can hardly be said to think; their notions are almost all adoptive; and, in general, I believe it is better that it should be so; as such common prejudices contribute more to order and quiet than their own separate reasonings would do, uncultivated and unimproved as they are.

Local prejudices prevail only with the herd of mankind, and do not impose upon cultivated, informed, and reflecting minds; but then there are notions equally false, though not so glaringly absurd, which are entertained by people of superior and improved understandings, merely for want of the necessary pains to investigate, the proper attention to examine, the penetration requisite to determine the truth. Those are the prejudices which I would have you guard against, by a manly exertion and attention of your reasoning faculty.

RELIGION.

ERRORS and mistakes, however gross, in matters of opinion, if they are sincere, are to be pitied; but not punished, nor laughed at. The blindness of the understanding is as much to be pitied as the blindness of the eyes: and it is neither laughable nor criminal for a man to lose his way in either case. Charity bids us endeavour to set him right by arguments and persuasions; but charity, at the same time, forbids us either to punish or ridicule his misfortune. Every man seeks for truth, but God only knows who has found it. It is unjust to persecute and absurd to ridicule people for their several opinions, which they cannot help entertaining upon the conviction of their reason. It is he who tells or acts a lie that is guilty, and not he who honestly and sincerely believes the lie.

The object of all public worships in the world is the same; it is that great Eternal Being who created every thing. The different manners of worship are by no means subjects of ridicule. Each sect thinks his own the best ; and I know no infallible judge in this world to decide which is the best.

EMPLOYMENT OF TIME.

How little do we reflect on the use and value of time ; it is in every body's mouth, but in few people's practice. Every fool, who slatterns away his whole time in nothings, frequently utters some trite commonplace sentence to prove, at once, the value and the fleetness of time. The sun-dials all over Europe have some ingenious inscription to that effect; so that nobody squanders away their time without frequently hearing and seeing how necessary it is to employ it well, and how irrevocable it is if lost. Young people are apt to think they have so much time before them that they may squander what they please of it, and yet have enough left; as great fortunes have frequently seduced people to a ruinous profusion. But all these admonitions are useless, where there is not a fund of good sense and reason to suggest rather than to receive them.

IDLENESS.—Time is precious, life short, and consequently not a single moment should be lost. Sensible men know how to make the most of time, and put out their whole sum either to interest or pleasure ; they are never idle, but continually employed either in amusements or study. It is a universal maxim, that idleness is the mother of vice. It is, however, certain, that laziness is the inheritance of fools, and nothing can be so despicable as a sluggard. · Cato, the censor, a wise and virtuous Roman, used to say there were but three actions of his life that he regretted : the first was the having revealed a secret to his wife ; the second, that he had once gone by sea when he might have gone by land ; and the third, the having passed one day *without doing any thing.*

READING.—'Take care of the pence ; for the pounds will take care of themselves,' was a very just and sensible reflection of old Mr. Lowndes, the famous secretary of the treasury under William III., Anne, and George I. I therefore recommend to you to take care of minutes ; for hours will take care of themselves. Be doing something or other all day long ; and do not neglect half-hours and quarters of hours, which, at the year's end, amount to a great sum. For instance, there are many short intervals in the day between studies and pleasures ; instead of sitting idle and yawning in those intervals, snatch up some valuable book, and continue the reading of that book till you have got through it ; never burden your mind with more than one thing at a time : and, in reading this book, do not run it over superficially, but read every passage twice over at least ; do not pass on to a second till you thoroughly understand the first, nor quit the book till you are master of the subject: for, unless you do this, you may read it through, and not remember the contents of it for a week. The books I would particularly recommend, amongst others, are the *Marchioness Lambert's Advice to her Son and Daughter, Cardinal Retz's Maxims, Rochefoucault's Moral Reflections, Bruyere's Characters, Fontenelle's Plurality of Worlds, Sir Josiah Child on Trade, Bolingbroke's Works*: for style, his *Remarks on the History of England*, under the name of Sir John Oldcastle ; *Puffendorf's Jus Gentium*, and *Grotius de Jure Belli et Pacis*; the last two are well translated by Barbeyrac. For occasional half-hours or less, read works of invention, wit and humour ; but never waste your minutes on trifling authors, either ancient or modern.

Nor are pleasures idleness, or time lost, provided they are the pleasures of a rational being; on the contrary, a certain portion of time employed in those pleasures is very usefully employed.

TRANSACTING BUSINESS.—Whatever business you have, do it the first moment you can; never by halves, but finish it without interruption, if possible. Business must not be sauntered and trifled with; and you must not say to it as Felix did to Paul, 'At a more convenient season I will speak to thee.' The most convenient season for business is the first; but study and business, in some measure, point out their own times to a man of sense; time is much oftener squandered away in the wrong choice and improper methods of amusement and pleasures.

METHOD.—Dispatch is the soul of business; and nothing contributes more to dispatch than method. Lay down a method for every thing, and stick to it inviolably, as far as unexpected incidents may allow. Fix one certain hour and day in the week for your accounts, and keep them together in their proper order; by which means they will require very little time, and you can never be much cheated. Whatever letters and papers you keep, docket and tie them up in their respective classes, so that you may instantly have recourse to any one. Lay down a method, also, for your reading, for which you allot a certain share of your mornings; let it be in a consistent and consecutive course, and not in that desultory and immethodical manner in which many people read scraps of different authors upon different subjects. Keep a useful and short commonplace book of what you read, to help your memory only, and not for pedantic quotations. Never read history without having maps and a chronological book of tables lying by you, and constantly recurred to; without which history is only a confused heap of facts.

You will say, it may be, as many young people would, that all this order and method is very troublesome, only fit for dull people, and a disagreeable restraint upon the noble spirit and fire of youth. I deny it; and assert, on the contrary, that it will procure you both more time and more taste for your pleasures; and, so far from being troublesome to you, that, after you have pursued it a month it would be troublesome to you to lay it aside. Business whets the appetite, and gives a taste to pleasures, as exercise does to food; and business can never be done without method: it raises the spirits for pleasures; and a *spectacle*, a ball, an assembly, will much more sensibly affect a man who has employed, than a man who has lost, the preceding part of the day; nay, I will venture to say, that a fine lady will seem to have more charms to a man of study or business than to a saunterer. The same listlessness runs through his whole conduct, and he is as insipid in his pleasures as inefficient in every thing else.

I hope you earn your pleasures, and consequently taste them; for, by the way, I know a great many who call themselves men of pleasure, but who in truth have none. They adopt other people's indiscriminately, but without any taste of their own. I have known them often inflict excesses upon themselves, because they thought them genteel; though they sat as awkwardly upon them as other people's clothes would have done. Have no pleasures but your own, and then you will shine in them.

Many people think that they are in pleasures, provided they are neither in study nor in business. Nothing like it: they are doing nothing, and might just as well be asleep. They contract habitudes from laziness, and they only frequent those places where they are free from all restraints and attentions. Be upon your guard against this idle profusion of time; and let every place you go to be either the scene of quick and lively pleasures or the school of your improvements; let every company you go into either gratify your senses, extend your knowledge, or refine your manners.

If, by accident, two or three hours are sometimes wanting.for some useful purpose, borrow them from your sleep. Six, or, at most, seven hours' sleep is, for a constancy, as much as you or any body can want; more is only laziness and dozing, and is both unwholesome and stupifying. If, by chance, your business or your pleasure should keep you up till four or five o'clock in the morning, rise exactly at your usual time, that you may not lose the precious morning hours, and that the want of sleep may force you to go to bed earlier the next night.

GUARD AGAINST FRIVOLOUSNESS.—Above all things, guard against frivolousness. The frivolous mind is always busied, but to little purpose: it takes little objects for great ones, and throws away upon trifles that time and attention which only important things deserve. Nicknacks, butterflies, shells, insects, &c., are the object of their most serious researches. They contemplate the dress, not the character, of the company they keep. They attend more to the decorations of a play than to the sense of it; and to the ceremonies of a court more than to its politics. Such an employment of time is an absolute loss of it.

To conclude this subject: Sloth, indolence, and effeminacy are pernicious, and unbecoming a young fellow; let them be your *resource* forty years hence, at soonest. Determine, at all events, and however disagreeable it may be to you in some respects, and for some time, to keep the most distinguished and fashionable company of the place you are at, either for their rank or for their learning, or *le bel esprit et le gout*. This gives you credentials to the best companies, wherever you go afterward.

Know the true value of time; snatch, seize, and enjoy every moment of it. No idleness, no laziness, no procrastination; never put off till to-morrow what you can do to-day. That was the rule of the famous and unfortunate pensionary De Witt; who, by strictly following it, found time not only to do the whole business of the republic, but to pass his evenings at assemblies and suppers, as if he had nothing else to do or think of.

VANITY.

BE extremely on your guard against vanity, the common failing of inexperienced youth, but particularly against that kind of vanity which dubs a man a coxcomb—a character which, once acquired, is more indelible than that of the priesthood. It is not to be imagined by how many different ways vanity defeats its own purposes. One man decides peremptorily upon every subject, betrays his ignorance upon many, and shews a disgusting presumption upon the rest; another desires to appear successful among the women: he hints at the encouragement he has received from those of the most distinguished rank and beauty, and intimates a particular connexion with some one: if it is true, it is ungenerous; if false, it is infamous: but, in either case, he destroys the reputation he wants to get. Some flatter their vanity by little extraneous objects, which have not the least relation to themselves; such as being descended from, related to, or acquainted with, people of distinguished merit and eminent characters. They talk perpetually of their grandfather Such-a-one, their uncle Such-a-one, and their intimate friend Mr. Such-a-one, whom, possibly, they are hardly acquainted with. But admitting it all to be as they would have it, what then? Have they the more merit for those accidents? Certainly not. On the contrary, their taking up adventitious, proves their want of intrinsic, merit; a rich man never borrows. Take this rule for granted, as a never-failing one, That you must never seem to affect the character in which you have a mind to shine. Modesty is the only sure bait, when you angle for praise. The affectation of courage will make even a brave man pass only for a bully; as the affectation of wit will make a man of parts pass for a coxcomb. By this modesty I do not mean timidity and awkward bashfulness. On the contrary, be inwardly firm and steady; know your own value, whatever it may be, and act upon that principle; but take great care to let nobody discover that you do know your own value. Whatever real merit you have, other people will discover; and the people always magnify their own discoveries, as they lessen those of others.

VIRTUE.

VIRTUE is a subject which deserves your and every man's attention. It consists in doing good and in speaking truth; the effects of it, therefore, are advantageous to all mankind, and to one's self in particular. Virtue makes us pity and relieve the misfortunes of mankind; it makes us promote justice and good order in society; and, in general, contributes to whatever tends to the real good of mankind. To ourselves it gives inward comfort and satisfaction, which nothing else can do, and which nothing else can rob us of. All other advantages depend upon others as much as upon ourselves. Riches, power, and greatness, may be taken away from us by the violence and injustice of others, or by inevitable accidents; but virtue depends only upon ourselves, and nobody can take it away from us. Sickness may deprive us of all the pleasures of the body; but it cannot deprive us of our virtue, nor of the satisfaction which we feel from it. A virtuous man, under all the misfortunes of life, still finds an inward comfort and satisfaction, which makes him happier than any wicked man can be with all the other advantages of life. If a man has acquired great power and riches by falsehood, injustice, and oppression, he cannot enjoy them, because his conscience will torment him, and constantly reproach him with the means by which he got them. The stings of his conscience will not even let him sleep quietly, but he will dream of his crimes; and, in the day-time, when alone, and when he has time to think, he will be uneasy and melancholy. He is afraid of every thing; for, as he knows mankind must hate him, he has reason to think they will hurt him if they can. Whereas, if a virtuous man be ever so poor and unfortunate in the world, still his virtue is its own reward, and will comfort him under all his afflictions. The quiet and satisfaction of his conscience make him cheerful by day and sleep sound at night: he can be alone with pleasure, and is not afraid of his own thoughts. Virtue forces her way, and shines through the obscurity of a retired life; and sooner or later, it always is rewarded.

To conclude:—Lord Shaftesbury says, that he would be virtuous for his own sake, though nobody were to know it; as he would be clean for his own sake, though nobody were to see him.

END OF THE PRINCIPLES OF POLITENESS.

CPSIA information can be obtained at www.ICGtesting.com
Printed in the USA
LVOW02s1312261013

358741LV00007B/199/P